KU-519-175

ADVENTURES
OF THE HORSE
DOCTOR'S
HUSBAND

ADVENTURES OF THE HORSE DOCTOR'S HUSBAND

FEATURING
· HIGHWAY ·
THE 1-75
MIRACLE HORSE

JUSTIN B. LONG

Copyright © 2019 Justin Boyd Long

All rights reserved. No portion of this publication may be reproduced, stored in a retrieval system, or transmitted by any means-electronic, mechanical, photocopying, recording, or any other-except for brief quotations in printed reviews, without the prior written permission of the publisher.

This is a work of creative nonfiction. The events are portrayed to the best of Justin B. Long's memory. While all the stories in this book are true, some names and identifying details have been changed to protect the privacy of the people and animals involved.

Published in the United States by Springhill Media
Newberry, Florida, USA
https://SpringhillEquine.com

SPRINGHILL

Cover & Book Design: mycustombookcover.com

Limits of Liability and Disclaimer Warranty:
The author shall not be liable for your misuse of this material. This book is strictly for entertainment purposes.

Orders by US trade bookstores and wholesalers: Please contact the publisher at the address above.

Printed in the United States of America

Library of Congress Control Number: 2019909112

ISBN: 978-1-948169-21-9 (paperback) 978-1-948169-22-6 (hardcover edition) 978-1-948169-20-2 (ebook)

First Edition

For Erica, who has made the
world a better place for horses, and their people

Other books by Justin B. Long, written under the pseudonym
J. Boyd Long

THE DIMWORLD SERIES
Genesis Dimension
When Good Plans Go Bad
Inside The Machine

Table of Contents

Forward

Just so that we're all on the same page, I want to tell you a few things about this book. These adventures really happened, but it's important to remember that these all happened with real people, and real animals. The horse world is relatively small, and I don't want anyone to feel that I am putting their laundry out for the world to see, or that their confidence in the privacy practices of our veterinary practice has been compromised. In that spirit, I have changed a lot of names and details. Perhaps the people who were involved in a particular situation might recognize their story, but that's about it.

Another thing I'd like to mention is that there are a lot of medical details that I did not include. My amazing wife

Erica is the doctor, not me, and I don't even know half of the things she is looking for when she glances at a horse. Some of the stuff I do know, but when I write it down, it turns an adventure story into a textbook of dense medical terminology, and that just sucks the fun right out of the story. So, please consider what you read here as entertainment, and not a step-by-step on veterinary medicine practices.

My goal in writing this down has been to share with you a glimpse of my life. I have new adventures all the time, some of which are not appropriate to share, and some of which are. I hope that you'll learn a few things, and have a few laughs, and maybe even be sad a few times. I find it fascinating to learn about things that are happening in the world all around us that we never see, and in the case of these stories, in the backyards of people right in our communities. So, relax and enjoy!

In the Beginning

I guess I should start by introducing myself and telling you a little bit about how I ended up with this amazing life filled with adventures. My name is Justin Long, and I'm an author, a business owner, and a podcaster, as well as a horse doctor's husband (a full-time occupation in its own right). My wife, Dr. Erica Lacher, is an equine veterinarian, and we own Springhill Equine Veterinary Clinic, which is a large-animal practice near Gainesville, Florida. I handle a lot of the administrative aspects of the business such as bookkeeping, paying bills, managing the website, recording and producing our podcast (Straight from the Horse Doctor's Mouth), and that sort of thing, as well as some of the other more exciting things that I'll be telling you about.

Back in 2014, I was living in an army town near the coast of Georgia called Hinesville. I was single, reasonably well-employed as a purchaser and inventory control specialist with an industrial equipment manufacturing company, and I was doing my best to live a full life. I was an active member of the local Arts Council, and my friend Tom and I were on a quest to see every state park in Georgia via motorcycle. I was dating on occasion, and generally happy. Through extensive discussions with my therapist, I knew what I was looking for in terms of a long-term relationship, but I was really losing hope in actually finding someone who met my criteria.

One day, after yet another fruitless search through the online dating world, I was expressing my frustrations to my best friend, Kristen.

"Why are you wasting time and money on these dating websites?" she asked. Kristen is very good about speaking her mind with me, which is invaluable.

"Where else am I going to find someone?" I countered. "I'm not going to find the right woman in a bar, since I don't drink anymore. The odds of running into the one person in three hundred million at a bookstore or an art class are proving to be extremely low. I don't know where else to look." Resignation filled my voice, as it always does when I'm facing an impossible barrier. "At least the dating sites are screening out all the ones who are NOT the one," I added, "which is all of them, so far."

"I know that, doofus," Kristen replied, with her usual tact and charm. "I'm saying, why waste your time and money on these hook-up sites? You're all about science and logic, so you need to get on eHarmony. It's the only one that does an actual personality profile and gives you scientific, psychologically probable matches. Also, because it's expensive, it weeds out all the people who aren't really serious about it."

She stumped me on that one. As much as I like to contradict her, I couldn't come up with anything at all.

"Well," I said at last, "you got me there. I guess it makes sense to go that route."

"Of course it does," she replied. "I'm always right." She paused for a moment, just to give me a bit of rope, which I wisely chose to ignore. "I know how hard it was for you to say that. I guess you have your big-boy pants on today."

I sighed, letting her have her moment.

"You know, the biggest problem I'm having is that people don't accurately represent themselves on these dating sites," I said. "They put up the description of who they want to be, instead of who they are."

"Look, just do this," Kristen said. "It'll cost the same as the next three dinner dates that are going to leave you disappointed anyway." Again, I couldn't refute her logic.

So it was that the last week in May of 2014, I sat down and took the personality profile. I was pleased to find that it was fairly extensive, and having recently taken the Myers-Briggs personality profile, I felt that eHarmony had done a pretty good job in their assessment. (I'm an INFJ/T, just for the record, except on days when I'm an INTJ/T. It's about 50/50 between the F and the T.) I was also pleased to find that there was not a lot of space on my profile for me to ad lib descriptions of myself, which meant that there were minimal opportunities for others to misrepresent themselves. I began to have a bit of hope.

A week later, eHarmony was still reporting that there was no one in the state of Georgia who was more than a 65% match for me. Again, I felt dejected.

"Why am I so hard to match up?" I asked Kristen. "I'm not a regular guy, but I'm sure there are lots of women out there who aren't looking for a regular guy, right?"

"Why are you so attached to Hinesville?" she countered. "You don't have any reason to stay there, or even in Georgia, for that matter. Expand your search and see if there are some matches somewhere else."

Again, she had me in a corner. I expanded the search to nationwide, mainly to prove to her that it wouldn't change anything. The one person who was compatible with me had probably lived and died a thousand years ago. With no expectations, and with only a tiny bit of hope, I checked out the results.

There were two solid matches. One was in Florida, and the other one was in Oregon. I checked out the one in Florida briefly before heading to work. She met my four basic criteria, which had never happened before (Doesn't drink, doesn't smoke, doesn't have or want kids, and not religious. [I'm not saying all people should be this way, that's just what I'm in to]). I really couldn't tell what she looked like, because she was wearing a helmet in every picture. One of them was her in a tree, wearing a helmet. The others were of her riding a horse and wearing a helmet. She was a doctor, which told me she was probably pretty bright, which was also important to me. I had to go to work, but I did so with a bounce in my step. There was a glimmer of hope on the horizon.

When I got home that night, I had an email from eHarmony, notifying me that the woman in Florida had sent me a smiley face. I assumed that was a good thing, and dug into her profile with serious enthusiasm. She seemed to be amazing and impressive, so I decided to write her a brief message.

> *Hi Erica, my name is Justin. I know that eHarmony wants us to start our communication with their pre-made questions instead of going straight to emailing, but I'm a bit of a rebel, and if you are as amazing as you seem to be, I don't want to waste a week going through the official channels. I hope that's not too forward! ~ Justin*

I sent the message, and it left me feeling giddy, terrified, and excited about possibilities. Filled with excess energy and emotion, I called Kristen to tell her all about this mystery woman who sent me a smile. I probably gushed on for at least ten minutes before she tried to take me down a notch.

"You can't act this way if and when you talk to her," Kristen cautioned me. "Don't overwhelm her right off the bat, or she'll freak out and run the other way."

"I know, I know," I said. "I felt that my message was very reserved."

"The fact that you sent it was not reserved," she pointed out. "You're supposed to do this question and answer thing for a week."

"Yeah, my therapist is going to tell me the same thing," I said. "I'm thirty-eight years old. I only have so many good days left, and I hate to waste a week of my life following protocols that were designed to keep twenty-year-old kids from getting married right away."

The next morning, I had another email from eHarmony. Erica had responded to my message:

Hi, Justin. I'll do you one better. Here's my phone number. I'll be in the truck all day, driving to Atlanta for a horse show. Call me.

I almost died. I considered calling in sick to work. I considered calling Kristen, who lives in California, three hours behind me. I considered re-paving the driveway and dancing on the roof. I considered that I could probably meet her in Macon and have lunch, but even in my ecstatic state, I realized that was probably a little rash. I finally decided it would be best to stay on schedule and went to the gym to swim laps.

I made it to work, but I couldn't focus on anything. I shuffled papers around and checked the clock every few seconds. When it was finally break time, I walked outside the office and dialed her number. My stomach was in knots, and I almost hung up the second it started ringing. She answered on the second ring.

"Hello?"

At this point, I realized that I had not written a script, or even jotted down some notes to go off, which is very unlike me. What should I say? I panicked, and almost hung up again. I had no idea how to have this conversation.

"Hi, Erica?" I asked, cursing the quiver in my voice. I have a very deep, strong voice, which is complimented regularly by people I talk to. Today it came out as a whimpering squeak as my throat tightened down in an effort to screw me over.

"Yes," she replied, calm and confident.

"Hi, this is Justin Long. From eHarmony. I'm the guy in Georgia. You sent me your phone number?"

"Yes, I know who you are," she laughed. "I don't just give my number out to a bunch of people on dating sites!"

"Oh, I didn't mean to insinuate that," I said, backpedaling and silently beating myself up. This was exactly why I should have written a script. "I was just. . ." My face felt like it was on fire, and my heart was hammering against my chest in a way that suggested something bad might happen if it kept that up much longer. I considered about a thousand possible things to say next, trying to find something that would not make me sound like an idiot. "So, what is a horse show in Atlanta like? What do you do?" It seemed like a safe way to get her talking for a moment so I could regroup.

"Oh, I do hunter jumpers," she said. I had no idea what that meant. "There's a big show in Atlanta every year where they had the Olympics back in '96."

"I feel a bit silly asking this," I said. "I lived on a cattle ranch in Wyoming when I was in high school, and my experience with horses consists of working cows and going to rodeos, but I haven't even been in that world for twenty years. I'm really not sure what you mean by hunter jumper."

"It's English riding, instead of western," she explained. "We jump the horses over fences, and try to go as fast as possible without knocking any of the rails down."

"Well, that explains the helmet in your horse picture," I said. "I've never seen people wear helmets on a horse before. In Wyoming, they wear cowboy hats."

"Well, aside from being the rule in our sport, I'm pretty attached to my head," she said. "I've seen enough head trauma injuries from people coming off a horse unexpectedly. I won't ride without one."

She explained the whole jumping thing to me, which did little to help my understanding of the sport, but did wonders for calming me down. I also learned that as a veterinarian, she worked primarily on horses, and owned her own practice. I grew more and more impressed with her as the conversation went on. She was very bright, articulate, and confident, which I liked very much.

"So, I've been talking about me for an hour," she said at last. "Tell me about you. What do you do? How did you go from a cattle ranch in Wyoming to Georgia?"

I told her all about my stint in the army, where I learned to operate heavy equipment like bulldozers, bucket loaders, and tractor-trailers, and how I was stationed at Ft. Stewart, Georgia.

"How long were you in the army?" she asked.

"Just three years," I said. "I knew right away that it wasn't the place for me. I can't have that many people in charge of me. After that I was an over-the-road truck driver for a year."

"Oh, you can drive a truck?" she asked. "And back a trailer?"

"I'm excellent at backing trailers," I said with some pride. "It's one of my many super-powers."

"You have no idea how excited that makes me," she said.

"Uh… hhmm," I stammered. "No one has ever been excited about that before. I'm not sure what to say."

"I have a twenty-eight-foot gooseneck horse trailer," she said. "The fact that you can handle that gives you some points. So, what did you do after you quit driving trucks?"

"Well, after I came off the road, I delivered propane for a few years, and then I went to Iraq as a civilian contractor and drove a truck over there for a while." I thought for a moment. "I probably didn't pick up a lot of useful skills with that stuff, but when I came back here, I got a job as a heavy equipment mechanic, working with the army. That gave me a lot of useful skills. When they laid off all the civilians a few years ago, I ended up here, working in the parts department. I've learned all about managing inventory, purchasing, and that stuff."

I told her about being in a band, and how I didn't have any furniture in my living room, just guitars and keyboards, speakers, and recording equipment. I told her about my love of painting, and some of the fun things I'd done with the arts council. I told her about my Honda GoldWing motorcycle, and how Tom and I were touring Georgia's state parks, trying to see all the waterfalls. At some point in the conversation, it occurred to me that my fifteen-minute break was probably over. I checked the time and was horrified to see that we had been on the phone for nearly two hours.

"Look, I hate to say this, but I should probably go make an appearance in my office," I said. "I just realized I haven't been there in two hours, and I probably have a hundred missed calls and emails to deal with."

We spent another ten minutes making plans for the next call, while getting sidetracked a few times. I finally got back to my office, which I shared with my supervisor.

"Where the hell did you go?" he asked. "I thought you quit!"

"Dude, I just spent the best two hours of my life meeting the woman I've been waiting for," I said.

"Oh, shit," he said, rolling his eyes. "You aren't going to be worth a damn for a week."

Little did he know how prophetic that remark would be. Two weeks, ten emails, and fifteen phone calls later, I made my first trip to Florida to meet Erica in person. I thought perhaps I had taken a wrong turn towards the end, as the dirt road I was on kept getting narrower and more overgrown, but at last it opened up in a beautiful lush green meadow. The driveway ended at a closed electric gate. Flustered, and still afraid I might not be in the right spot, I called her.

"Hi," I said. "I think I'm here. Is there a big black gate on your drive?"

"Yep," she said. "Come on in."

"Uh, how do I open the gate?" I asked, feeling dense. I clearly had no experience with gated driveways, and I was afraid that might say something negative about me, but I would soon learn that the gate is about keeping the horses in rather than keeping the world out.

"Push the button beside you," she said. I could hear her laughing at me.

I looked out my window, and sure enough, there was a box on a pole right there, with a single button on it. I pushed the button, and the gate began to swing open.

"Okay, I feel like an idiot," I told her. "I should have looked around for at least a nanosecond before announcing myself as unobservant."

She was still laughing at me as I pulled up and parked. The building was a big beige concrete block barn, with wooden stairs going up one end to a huge porch overlooking the pastures and the forests beyond. I looked around for a moment, noting a variety of flowering plants and bushes, before climbing out. Two dogs met me at the truck door, a pit bull and a Jack Russell. I quickly commenced to making their acquaintance with some scratching and fussing as Erica came down the stairs.

"It looks like you've met Norma and Rachel," she said with a grin. "Don't give them too much attention, or they'll never leave you alone."

It was strange meeting her in person. I felt like I had known her forever by now, but I still hadn't seen a picture of her without a helmet on. She was short (as most people seem to me, since I'm six feet, two inches tall) and curvy, which I tried very hard not to admire too closely as she took me on a tour. I liked the way her shoulder-length brown ponytail bounced as she walked. We started in the barn, where she made introductions.

"This is Clu, Ernie, and Vespa," she said, pointing to each horse in their stall. "On this side is Sydney, Gigi, and Angie." She nodded at a white cat as it strolled through. "That's Pesca. Out in the back field is Millie, who is the mother of Vespa, Gigi, and Angie. The donkey out there with her is Pet."

My head reeled with names, most of which I was forgetting faster than I could even process. We went upstairs, where she introduced me to a few more cats. I decided I was going to need to make an animal name matrix if I was ever going to have any hope of learning who was who.

We went to dinner at a local pizza place called Villagios. I learned that she was all about local restaurants rather than national chains, which greatly appealed to me. She was also a voracious reader, and very much an outdoorsy person. I asked her about the picture of her in a tree, wearing a helmet and hanging from a rope and harness.

"Norma Jean, the Jack Russell, chased Ofeibea, one of the white cats, up a tree one time. It was one of the big live oaks behind the barn, on the edge of the woods. She went all the way to the top, of course." She paused for a drink. "I spent hours trying to get her down, couldn't do it. She wouldn't budge. It was going to be dark in a few hours, and I didn't want her to be up there all night, so I Googled 'cat rescue' and found this guy named Danny. He came out with all these ropes and harnesses, like rock climbing equipment. He threw a rope over a branch, and climbed the rope. He reset the rope on a higher branch and climbed it again, and was almost up to the cat when she realized the gig was up. She climbed down on her own, and he rappelled down. I was like, 'Damn, that looks fun!' I found out he does sport tree climbing too, in addition to cat rescue. I went and tried it out with my best friend, and it was great. I ended up buying some gear and now I climb trees. Really, it's more rope climbing than tree climbing, but whatever. I like it."

The whole weekend went by in a flash. We got to know each other through a million stories while she showed me around the Gainesville area. I told her about being an artist and showed her pictures of my paintings, and we went to the art museum. She told me she liked my paintings better than most of the ones they had on display, which made me feel pretty good. I really enjoyed sitting in the rocking chairs on her porch and watching the horses graze. It was very serene and quiet. She lived in a wonderful, mostly secluded paradise. I decided to come back as often as she would let me.

Back in Georgia, I started taking my vacation days, one almost every Friday. I would take my things to work on Thursday and leave as early as possible for the three-hour drive to Florida, where I would stay until Sunday afternoon. Sometimes she would come up to Georgia, and we would mess around in Savannah, or ride the motorcycle to a state park somewhere. After seven or eight months of this, we both knew it was time for me to move to Florida.

"I don't want you to leave," she said one Sunday afternoon. We had spent the weekend at a horse show, which I was becoming much more familiar with. "I really like it so much better when you're here." She hugged me, then added, "And not just because you're a badass truck driver and I can relax in the passenger seat, either."

I grinned. "You better be careful talking like that," I said. "One of these days I'm going to show up with a truck full of guitars and speakers and paintings and some clothes. Then you won't ever get me to leave!"

"So, when is that going to happen?" she asked, calling my bluff. "Next week? I'm ready when you are."

It happened just like that. That's the way it is with her: no drama, no complications. I started applying for jobs in Gainesville.

"Why don't you work at the vet clinic?" she asked me one day. "You know how to do a lot of different things. You can do the bookkeeping, pay bills, fix things, and do all the stuff I end up doing to keep the business going. That would let me see more horses and do less office stuff."

I didn't even really consider it. "No, that's a bad plan," I said. "We'd end up spending too much time together and start driving each other crazy. It never works out."

She didn't press me then, but the more weeks went by, and the more jobs I didn't get, the more I started thinking about it. Finally, I brought the subject back up.

"So, how would it work?" I asked one day. "I'd need a lot of training to do some of that stuff."

"Mish will help you out with that," she said. Mish was her best friend and the bookkeeper I would be replacing so she could focus on her regular job.

We hammered out the details sufficiently, so that I felt confident enough to put in my notice at my job.

"I knew it!" Zach, my supervisor, cackled. "I knew you'd be moving down there." He slapped his leg, laughing. "She done got you all wrapped up," he said.

"Yep, that she does," I agreed. "That she does."

"Well, I'm glad you found the one," he said, being serious for a moment. "I hate like hell to lose you. You been doing your job and half of mine for two years. Hell, I'm gonna have to start working around here." We both laughed, and I felt better about quitting. He was one of the rare people that I felt really appreciated me.

On our nine-month anniversary, I pulled her horse trailer up to Georgia, and we loaded all my worldly possessions into it, or at least the ones that were going to Florida. Erica was excited about the king size pillow-top mattress, which was a vast improvement over her aging queen size bed. We spent a few days figuring out how to merge our household items, and I gave the rest away to friends and neighbors.

The move to Florida improved my quality of life in ways I never could have imagined. My therapist was ecstatic for me, despite being concerned that I was moving too fast. Kristen was a bit concerned about that too, but I consoled myself with the knowledge that if I waited ten years, it would still be too fast for either of them.

I really liked the new home front, of course, but I liked the area, too. I also liked my new job. I didn't know what I was doing, but working for a small business gave me a much better sense of purpose than working for a giant conglomerate. Everything I did mattered all of a sudden. The decisions I made affected the whole business, and I could see how my ideas made things better or worse. With a total of eight people in the company, I really felt like my efforts were visible, rather than being one invisible guy in a company with thousands of employees. I liked it!

My relationship with Erica continued to get better and better. We would joke about liking each other so much that we might even consider getting married, even though both of us had sworn to our friends and family in the past that we would never get married. At some point, it wasn't a joke anymore, though neither of us knew when that exact moment occurred. It just evolved.

"I sure do like you a lot," I told her one afternoon. We had just returned from a canoe trip, and were looking at the pictures we had taken. "I mean, if I was the kind of guy that would get married, I would totally marry you."

"Hhmmm," she smiled, wrapping her arms around me and looking up into my eyes. "I like you, too. If I was to ever make an exception to my rule about not getting married, it would have to be with someone as amazing as you."

"You know, there are probably only three or four guys as amazing as me on the whole planet, and they're either ninjas or astronauts, and definitely not the marrying kind." I puffed up my chest and put on my fake modesty face. "I'm not saying I'm a big deal, but... I'm kind of a big deal."

"Yeah, you're my big deal," she laughed.

Later that night at supper, we talked about things that needed to get done at the clinic the next day and the topic came up again.

"You know, I could take a lot of these phone calls off your plate if we were married," I said. "The only reason you have to talk to these people is because you're the business owner, and they won't talk to an employee. Maybe we should just call them all and tell them I'm your husband; tell them to put me on the 'Safe to Talk to' list."

"Well, you'd save some money on your taxes, too," Erica's mother said. She's a CPA and a business consultant, so I paid attention when she said things like that. "If you actually got married, that is."

"It would make it less awkward to introduce you to people on emergencies in the middle of the night," Erica said. "I mean, *husband* does sound more professional than *boyfriend*."

"I just can't imagine you in a wedding dress," I joked to Erica. I think her entire dress collection consisted of two dresses, both of which I had yet to see her wear.

"Oh, I wouldn't wear a dress," Erica said. "It would have to be a costume wedding or something."

And thus, the plan was hatched. That conversation started a ball rolling that resulted in the most memorable wedding of all time. We decided that in addition to us being in costume, everyone at the wedding would have to be in costume. Sticking to her non-traditionalist values, Erica also decided that she wasn't walking down the aisle. Instead, the wedding would be under a giant live oak tree in our back yard, and she would rappel out of the tree down to the altar. I was totally down with that.

We decided to keep it small, and low budget. Erica chose the character of Lara Croft, Tomb Raider. She went all out with combat boots, pistols, boot knife, and of course, the appropriate black shorts and halter top. Her entrance song was to be *The Imperial March*, from *Star Wars*.

I decided to be King Arthur from *Monty Python and the Search for the Holy Grail*, and my entrance music was the Vienna Philharmonic's rendition of *Fanfare*. Being committed to authenticity, I got real chain mail, a sword, and a crown. With the help of a friend with a sewing machine, we made a tunic with the mustached-sun face on it.

Erica's best friend Mish was her maid of honor, and she made a banana spider costume. It was perfect, as she also wanted to rappel out of the tree. Kristen flew out from California and was my "best man." She dressed as a Jedi Knight, complete with cloak and light saber.

The audience was the most bizarre mix of costumes ever assembled. So many people really embraced the idea of dressing up and came with amazing costumes. There was Pharaoh and Cleopatra, Little Bo Peep, people from *Star Wars* and *Star Trek*, superheroes, pirates, wenches, Bonnie and Clyde, Indiana Jones, Curious George and the Man in the Yellow Hat, and the list goes on.

Erica's uncle Bill performed the ceremony, in the character of Gandalf. He was a bit resistant to the bizarre concept of our ceremony at first, but by the time he took his place in front of the crowd, he understood that while we were having fun with the wedding, we were taking our relationship very seriously. He ended up embracing his role more than anyone else in the wedding party.

"Ladies and gentlemen," he cried out, raising his arms.

His gray robe and tall, pointed hat complemented his tall stature, and presented an impressive and believable wizard. "I bring you greetings from all the hobbits of the Shire! I bring you tidings from the elves, and from the House of Elrond himself!"

The crowd hushed. Erica and Mish were already in the tree, thirty feet above Gandalf, with the ropes pulled up and coiled beside them on the branches. I was in the barn aisle with Kristen, waiting and watching.

"Before I continue," Gandalf said, "I will step aside for a moment for a few remarks from Batman."

Batman strode to the front of the audience, pulled out a piece of paper, and cleared his throat.

"I would like to share with you a few words that were spoken at another wedding, from another time," he said. "This excerpt is from the movie, *The Princess Bride.*"

He cleared his throat again, as a few giggling people in the audience guessed what he was about to say.

"Mawwaige. Mawwaige is what bwings us togeveh today. Mawwaige, that bwessed awaingement, that dweam wiffin a dweam. And wuv, twu wuv, will fowwow you forevah, so tweashu your wuv."

He folded the paper and strode back to his seat. The people who were familiar with the movie laughed hysterically and applauded, while the other half who had not seen the movie (to include my mother) sat in a sort of stunned silence. That was even funnier than the presentation itself. Uncle Bill resumed his position.

I couldn't hear everything he said, as Kristen and I were laughing about the variety of reactions in the crowd. I started paying attention again just in time to hear my cue.

"And so, I call forth King Arthur!" Gandalf raised his arms, and the trumpets belted out the opening notes of *Fanfare*. In that moment, I was very glad I had all the sound equipment from the band, as the huge speakers were perfect for this event.

I looked at Kristen, who was sweating profusely in her Jedi costume. Even though it was late October, it was still hot and humid. "Are you ready?"

She nodded and held up the halved coconut shells. I began my entrance, pretending to ride a horse, with my head held high and proud. Kristen followed behind me, clapping the coconut shells together. It made a very realistic hoof clopping sound. As we made our way sedately to the front, I noticed again a division in the crowd: those that knew what I was doing, and those that didn't. I struggled to keep a straight face.

"Welcome, King Arthur!" Gandalf made a slight bow as the audience clapped. "Welcome!"

I wish I could tell you what he said after that, but to be totally honest, I don't really know. I realized that I was getting married, and that I was marrying Erica Lacher, the most impressive and awesome person I have ever met. I got so excited and emotionally overwhelmed with that thought that I almost started crying. I came back to the moment as Gandalf stepped aside and gestured above him.

"Is there a woman, a tree nymph, in all of this land who could be the wife of this great man?" he asked. That wasn't how we had it scripted, but Uncle Bill was on a roll by this point.

A coiled rope dropped out of the tree canopy and hit the ground with a thump. At the same time, the *Imperial March* began to pour out of the speakers, which added a ton of dramatic effect to the moment. Mish, in the form of a giant banana spider complete with pool noodle legs, came down the rope. Her back was to the audience, and she stopped halfway down and began twitching her leg in an effort to turn around. The crowd laughed appreciatively, and she finally made it the rest of the way down. She quickly removed her harness, as a second rope dropped to the ground.

Erica rappelled out of the tree like a total badass. She came down fast, with one leg kicked out in front of her, and an arm stuck out behind her. She was bristling with pistols and knives and hardware. I let out a whooping cheer. Apparently, that was all everyone else was waiting for, because a second later, the crowd let out a deafening roar of approval. She landed perfectly, and Mish helped her out of the harness, like they had practiced. A moment later she joined me.

If the part before that was a blur for me, everything after that was a complete flash. I looked at her, and she looked at me, and Gandalf said a bunch of things. She read me the vows she wrote, and I read her the vows I wrote. I got choked up in the middle of mine, but it worked out okay. I do remember the moment when she looked up from her paper and locked eyes with me.

"I choose you," she said.

I cried, but only for a second. At some point it was over, and we got to kiss. Finally, we turned to face the crowd as the theme song from *2001: A Space Odyssey* played. They screamed and cheered and cried and threw popcorn at us as we walked slowly to the back. I felt like I was in a dream. My heart was pounding, my cheeks were flushed, and I had a hard time focusing on any one thing. It was a strange feeling, but the good kind of strange.

So, that's the condensed version of how I became the husband of a horse doctor, and began a new life filled with adventure and excitement. For example, I've gone to the office to pick up some paperwork, and ended up assisting in a surgery on a horse. I've gone to get the bank deposit and ended up helping to hold a baby zebra still so it could get vaccinated. I've been woken up in the middle of the night to help Erica sew up a horse that ripped his leg open. I don't know about you, but that kind of stuff never used to happen to me!

2

Honey's New Year's Eve Bash

It's almost like horses know when it's a holiday, and that's when they seem to injure themselves in spectacular fashion. I don't know if this is a malicious thing, like they want to screw up the holiday for their owner, or if it's a self-preservation thing, like they know someone will be home to rescue them. It's hard to say. If I were a horse, it would probably be some of both, but that's just me.

On New Year's Eve, we got a call from a woman named Lisa who was crying, and seemed to be pretty sure that one of her horses was about to die. Erica had a hard time understanding her, but we at least knew who it was and where they were, and that something was wrong with the horse's leg. We left the house immediately and arrived about 4 pm at a small farm out in the woods near Trenton, Florida.

"I think she said it was one of the horses at her brother-in-law's house," Erica said as we pulled into the driveway. "It was hard to make out what she was saying. She keeps two of her horses here, and the rest at her house down the road, so if there isn't anyone here, we'll run on over there."

The house was a brown doublewide trailer, with a large covered porch built on to the back side, away from the road. It was covered by a stunning massive live oak tree, and there were several more live oaks of impressive size behind the house. As we passed the house, I saw a workshop and a few small storage buildings, but no barn.

"I'm assuming the horses live in a field?" I ventured. "I don't see a barn."

"Yeah, keep going around these trucks, and we should see someone," she said. "It looks like there're a lot of people here anyway, so we should find out something in a second."

There were about ten cars and trucks in the driveway, and once I passed them, I could see some kids staged along what I guessed was the route we had to drive to get to the horse. The first one was waving at us, confirming that we were in the right place. I rolled down the window as we approached her.

"Howdy," I said. "Is this where the sick horse is?"

"Hi," the girl replied. She looked to be about ten, and was hopping back and forth from one foot to the other. "Honey's hurt, not sick. Drive over there, and my sister will open the gate for you and show you where she is."

She turned around and took off running, and I drove toward the girl at the gate, which led into a semi-wooded pasture. She opened it as we got close, shooing away a couple of goats. I guessed that she was about twelve. She was wearing jeans tucked into a pair of bright pink rubber boots, and a pink t-shirt with a glitter horse on it.

"If you turn left and go around that white shed over there, you can park behind it," she said. "You'll see my cousin over there at the hole in the fence, and that's where you have to go through to get to Honey."

"Okie dokie," I replied.

I drove slowly, trying not to run over anything in the tall grass that might puncture a tire. Once we rounded the corner of the shed, I could see a cluster of people on the other side of a falling-down barbed wire fence. They were among a copse of small oak and pine trees.

"It looks like we're crashing a holiday party," I said. "We should have brought some noise makers, or snacks, or something. Of course, it seems to be primarily pre-teen horse girls, so I'd probably feel a bit out of place."

"Yeah, I don't think you're going to be part of that party," Erica agreed. "You don't have anything pink or camouflage on, and you're about thirty years too old to understand anything they say, or like their music."

The goats had followed us and were waiting patiently outside my door as I parked and got out. As promised, another teenage girl waited for us at an opening in the fence. The goats sniffed my legs for a second, then trotted over to the fence and tried to get past the girl guarding the opening.

"She's this way," the girl said. She seemed to be tasked with keeping the goats out, which was a full-time job from what I could see. She was very skinny, and I thought that the giant camouflage jacket she was wearing probably made her look like a weird bush with blonde hair to the goats.

"Okay, we're just going to grab some supplies, and we'll be right there," Erica said.

I opened the lift gate, and she quickly gathered the bandaging supplies and suture materials. We headed through the fence and over towards the group of people. As we approached, they moved back to let us in.

A palomino mare was standing there on three legs. The fourth leg was wrapped in blood-soaked Vet Wrap, which is similar to an Ace bandage. The leg was shaking and hanging awkwardly, and I realized that most of the people had been supporting the horse to help her stand. There appeared to be three generations of family here. The grandmother, a stout woman with short red hair in her early sixties, was holding the horse's head. Two heavyset women who were pretty clearly her daughters were there, a man I guessed was the husband of one of them, and a myriad of kids. Lisa, the daughter that owned the horse, explained the situation.

"Honey didn't come in for breakfast this morning," she began. "I didn't find that out until we got here this afternoon for the cookout, and I came out to look for her. Somehow, she got through the fence and came in here. She managed to get her foot stuck in this big vine, and she couldn't get it back out. When I found her, she was bleeding really bad, sweating, and shaking like a leaf. I don't know how long she's been here. We cut the vine away, but she can't walk, and she won't lie down. We got the hose over here and washed the leg off, like you said in your Facebook video a few weeks ago. She's got a puncture, and a lot of scrapes. Plus, she's not putting any weight on her leg, so I think it's broken."

Her face turned red, and tears coursed down her cheeks. I could feel the sadness radiating off of them, a wave of raw emotion. A few of the younger girls began sniffling and sobbing, and their swollen, red faces showing that it wasn't the first time that day.

"Is she going to die?" a little girl asked. She couldn't have been more than six or seven. Her huge blue eyes glinted with tears.

"Not if I can help it," Erica said. "Let me take a look at her and see what's going on."

She pulled the bandage scissors out and cut away the sodden, bloody wrap. The worst of the damage was between the elbow and the knee. It looked like something had gouged a hole through the muscle.

"Justin, I need the x-ray out of the truck," Erica said.

As I took off, I could hear her complimenting their response to the situation with the water hose and the support. They must have had ten water hoses put together to reach that far, and I hoped they had the same number of extension cords. Lisa's husband was managing that problem as I grabbed the three lead-lined aprons, and the two big cases that housed the radiograph machine, then quickly returned to the horse while dodging the goats at the fence.

"Alright," I said, setting everything down. "I need a volunteer, someone who doesn't plan on having children."

Instantly, all the teenage girls stepped back. The grandmother spoke up.

"Well, I guess that's me."

"That's perfect," I said. "I need you to hold her head, which you're already doing. I'm just going to have you put this apron on, and we'll shoot some X-rays. I'm Justin, by the way."

"I'm Sandra," she said. "Are you a doctor, too?"

"Oh, no," I laughed. "I'm the night and weekend technician. I just drive the truck and carry the heavy stuff around. I'm Dr. Lacher's husband, so I got the job by default."

"I see," she smiled. "Well, it's an important job, even if she gets all the glory."

"That's right," I said. "I'm not much of a spotlight kind of guy, anyway."

A few minutes later we had electricity. Erica finished setting up the radiograph, and we got to work taking images. I held the plate behind Honey's leg at various positions, and Erica shot the images. The girls watched intently as the x-rays showed up on the laptop screen, fascinated by the whole process. Suddenly, a goat wandered up and sniffed Honey's leg.

"Well, hello goat," I said. "Where did you come from?"

"Somebody get Little Bit out of here," Lisa shouted. "And get the other two horses out of here too, before we end up with all three of them hurt! Jamie, you're supposed to be over there at the fence keeping them out!"

"I wanted to see what was happening," Jamie said.

"You've got to guard the hole in the fence," Lisa said. "You need to let Dr. Lacher get in and out, but keep the goats and horses on the outside. We've got enough problems as it is."

Jamie and the girl in pink, who I figured out was Sissy, took off to get the goat and the horses put back on the other side of the fence. That proved to be a challenge, as all of the excitement was clearly inside where we were, and the other goats came in to see what we were doing. Don, Lisa's husband, ended up carrying one of the goats, and they finally got everyone away from Honey.

Erica finished taking images, and went through them one by one, explaining what she was looking for in each one. I put the radiograph machine away while she did that.

"First and foremost, we don't have any broken bones," she said. "That's great news. The way she's standing and holding that leg up is called a Dropped Elbow, and that usually means they've got a broken bone. In her case, I think it's because she's in a lot of pain, and she's exhausted because she can't get off her other three legs. She's afraid to lie down because she doesn't think she can get back up.

"She's got a lot of damage to her veins and nerves, but that stuff is secondary, at this point. We're going to bandage her up, manage her for pain and infection, and basically try to stabilize her enough that we can get her moved to a stall somewhere. She'll need to rest and get some strength back."

Tension drained out of the group so visibly that it would have been funny if it weren't such a serious situation. I realized that this family had been holding this horse up for an hour or more, all the while believing that she was going to die at the end of it. They had been on one hell of an emotional roller coaster.

"How are we going to move her?" Lisa asked.

"Once we get her bandaged up, we're going to duct tape a two by four to her leg and make a splint so she can hobble without putting all of her weight on her foot. If there's a stall here that we can get her in, I'm fine with that, at least for tonight."

"I've got some portable panels," Don said. "I can build her a stall right there in that clear spot, if that will help."

"That works for me," Erica said. "Basically, I want her to be in a place where she feels safe enough to lie down and rest. Tomorrow we can get her to wherever she's going to be until we get her healed up."

Lisa took charge of the situation and started putting people to work.

"Alright, you run to our house and get the panels," she said to Don. "Sissy, you go find your dad and tell him we need a two by four and a roll of duct tape. You girls, go start pulling up all the weeds over there, and make a clear spot. Oh, Don, bring a few bags of bedding back with you. We're going to need some light out here, too. I'm going to stay out here with the horse all night, so I'll need a blanket and a chair or something."

"I'll stay out here with you," Sandra said.

"And I want to get her to our house as soon as possible," Lisa added. "We can take better care of her over there."

People scattered and went to work. Erica and I got busy cleaning and bandaging the wounds. I made several trips to the truck to get things, as well as to put things away when we were done with them. Darkness was setting in fast, and I didn't want to lose anything in the pasture. By the time we were done bandaging and giving shots, the kids were back with a board and a roll of tape.

"All I could find was Hello Kitty duct tape," the older one explained. "I hope that's okay."

"I bet that will work perfect," Erica said, taking the tape and the board. "Okay, I'm going to need some extra hands. I need someone to hold the board and a few people to hold her leg as straight as you can while I wrap the tape around it."

Everyone lent a hand, and I stood back and took a few pictures as Erica taped the makeshift splint together.

I realized in that moment that Erica had taken a group of people who were grieving the expected loss of a loved one and given them hope, given them purpose, and given them an active role in saving the life of their horse. That was a pretty powerful moment for me.

"Alright, now we're ready for the hard part," Erica announced. "We've got to teach her to walk with this splint. We have to show her that she can trust it and put some weight on it. We're going to move super-slow, and we'll probably have to stop and re-tape it a few times."

"You tell us where you want us," Lisa said.

"We're going to put someone on each side of her by her flanks, to keep her back end pointed in the right direction. We'll keep Sandra on the halter pointing her head in the right direction, I'll help her move the leg and the splint. I need someone to watch the tape and tell me if it starts to tear or get loose."

We all took our positions. Erica lifted the splinted leg and moved it forward, then we all clucked and pushed and coaxed, and at last Honey took a shuddering step forward, placing some weight on the splint for a brief moment.

"Yay!" I cheered. The girls immediately followed suit, giving Honey a lot of reward and applause.

We went through the process again, and after a few tries she managed to take another step. We paused to let her rest and Erica added some tape to a few spots that were threatening to loosen up.

"We'll let her rest for a bit," she said, standing up. "I'm hoping that if we leave her alone a minute, she'll lean on the splint and give her other leg a rest."

Lisa went up to check on the weed-pulling progress and

Don drove up with the portable fence panels a moment later. I went to help him unload them and we quickly constructed a stall around the cleared area.

"That's a good girl," Erica exclaimed.

Everyone's head turned toward Honey. She was leaning fully on the splint and had lifted her front left leg up. She was shaking, but the relief of getting off of that leg was evident in her shining eyes and soft knickers.

"She's figuring out the splint," Erica said with a grin. "She's a quick learner!"

"Oh, she's sharp," Sandra said. "She picks up on stuff pretty fast. Sometimes that gets her in to trouble, but it's paying off for her today!"

"Oh, I know what you mean," I said with a laugh. "We've got a donkey that's too smart to stay out of trouble sometimes."

We gathered back around, and after a few more minutes of rest, we started easing her forward again. Now that she trusted the splint to hold her up, she moved a little easier. By the time we got her to the pen, there was bedding down, a water bucket in the corner, a hay bag full of alfalfa, and a feed bucket with supper in it hanging on the rail. There was also portable lighting being set up.

"You've got a pretty good team here," I said. "They really know how to get things done."

"They're kind of like Honey," Sandra said. "Sometimes they're great and sometimes they're too smart for their own good!"

We got Honey inside the pen and rearranged the feed and water so that she could reach it all without having to move. She had a large appetite, which is always a good sign. Leg injuries like this are dangerous for several reasons. One reason is that horses do most of their resting while standing, and they switch between their legs so that one is resting while they stand on the other three. If one leg isn't weight-bearing, they can't rest the other legs, and that will cause major complications, and can kill them.

"Okay," Erica said, stepping over to the fence by Lisa. "I think we've got her in a pretty good place for tonight. Aren't you glad you live in Florida? I think the low for tonight is about sixty, and that's probably about the best New Year's Eve temperature in the country."

"Oh my God, I know!" Lisa laughed. "Can you imagine having to do this if it was like ten degrees and snowing?"

"Not me," Erica said. "There's a reason I live in Florida."

"So, how long should we leave the splint on?" Lisa asked.

"I'd like to keep it on her for a few hours, as long as she acts okay with it," Erica said. "My goal is that she'll be able to rest her other legs enough by leaning on it. That way when you take it off, she'll go ahead and lie down. That's when she'll really start to recover. It's hard because the weaker she is, the less likely she is to lie down, even though that's what she needs to do. It's that survival mechanism. She knows that if she gets attacked by coyotes while she's down, that she won't have the energy to stand up. She just won't lie down if she doesn't feel strong enough."

"Okay, we can do that," Lisa said. "She's eating good, so that ought to help her build her strength."

"Absolutely," Erica said. "Now then, for tomorrow. You want to try to get her moved to your house, right?"

"Right," Lisa said. "We've got our barn finished now, so I can put her in a stall with good walls for her to lean on. Do you think she'll be able to get in a trailer and stand up for the ride?"

"I'll come back in the morning, and we'll check her out first to be sure," Erica said. "We'll change the bandage, and if she feels good, we'll help you get her loaded and moved."

"I can't thank you enough for all of this," Lisa said. Her eyes welled up with tears once again, but this time they were tears of relief. "This has been an unbelievably bad day, and I feel like you just swept in here and made it all better." She wrapped Erica up in a hug.

"She's lucky to have you for a mom," Erica said, hugging her back. "You did all the right things at all the right times."

"Well, I owe you for that too, since I learned it from your videos," Lisa laughed, wiping her eyes. "You're an amazing teacher."

"You really are," Sandra agreed, giving Erica a hug of her own. "We just love you to death!"

We headed home to feed our own horses, and get the barn cleaned. Erica and Lisa texted back and forth a few times throughout the evening, checking in and answering questions. The next morning, we headed back out. When we arrived, I was impressed with what they had done. There was a canopy set up next to the pen, and two of those deck chairs that lay out flat for sun tanning were under it, with blankets and pillows. They had a light, a cooler, and a table-all the comforts of home.

"Good morning and Happy New Year!" I called as we walked up.

"Good morning," Lisa replied. "Welcome back!"

"How did she do?" Erica asked, walking over to the edge of the pen to look at Honey.

"Well, we took the splint off about ten last night," Lisa said. "She kept acting like she was going to lie down, but she never actually did. We put the splint back on about midnight, and then took it back off about six this morning. She still hasn't lain down, but she isn't shaking anymore, so I feel better about her. She did a lot of eating and drinking, and she pooped a couple of times."

"Okay," Erica said. "She looks pretty good, even if she didn't get off her feet. Let me grab some stuff. We'll get her bandage changed and see what she looks like."

Erica cut away the bandage, and we all gathered around to look at her leg. The wound went down in layers. Near the edge, the hair was rubbed away from the skin. Closer inside the skin was gone and you could see the muscle. Through the hole in the muscle the damaged nerves and veins were visible.

"Okay, I'm going to stick a needle in the base of her leg to make sure we still have good blood flow," Erica said. "There's a lot of damage there, and I need to make sure she's getting enough blood to her foot."

She stuck a needle in just above the hoof line. I put my hand on Honey's muzzle and scratched her lightly to distract her. I held the halter with my other hand, but she made no effort to move away from the needle.

Blood dripped out of the shaft of the needle almost immediately. Erica tested a few more spots around her foot and they all produced the same result.

"Okay, that's fantastic," she announced. "She's getting plenty of blood past the wound, so that's one less thing we have to worry about."

"Well, that's good news," Lisa said. "As a matter of fact, that's the best news I've had since mom said she was going to get us some coffee!"

We laughed and Erica began putting on a new bandage.

"I think she's going be okay to move," she said. "Does your horse trailer have a ramp, or is it a step?"

"It's a step," Lisa said. "I think they've got a ramp here that we can use, though. It's one of those like you have on a U-Haul truck. We ought to be able to get her up that pretty easy."

"Oh, that's perfect," Erica said. "It won't be very steep, and they have some tread on them so she shouldn't slide around on it."

Lisa pulled out her phone and made a few calls to arrange everything.

"Okay, they're going to bring the ramp down here, and Don is on his way with the truck and trailer," she announced. "We should be ready to load her in about twenty minutes."

While we waited on Don, we helped them tear down the camp. Lisa's nephew showed up with some shears. He began moving the fence and clearing tree limbs so that the trailer could be backed right up to the pen. Just like the night before, they all worked as a team. By the time we had everything ready, the trailer was in place, and the ramp set.

"Okay, we're going to start off without the splint," Erica said. "If she can't do it, we'll stop and put it on her. We're going to go nice and slow, just like we did last night. Everybody ready?"

We took the end panel off the pen, and they began leading her out. It was about ten feet to the ramp, which was as close as they could get without hitting a serious tree branch. Honey moved much more confidently this morning, although she still lurched through the process of putting weight on her sore leg. We stopped at the base of the ramp to let her rest.

"I can't believe she's walking this well," Lisa said. "That's amazing."

"Well, it's 30% pain medication, 30% rest, and 40% tough horse," Erica said. "She's got a lot of fight in her."

We began inching up the ramp. Honey was not very confident in it. It was bowing under her weight and I didn't blame her for being nervous. I wasn't very confident in it either. It held strong though, and within another minute she was safely inside the trailer.

"Alright," Lisa said. "Mom, I need you to ride in here with her. Jamie and Sissy, you two ride with her too, and help her stand up if she starts to lean. Bobby, you ride in here and hold the ramp up against the wall so it doesn't fall over on her. I'm only going to drive about ten miles an hour. Does one of you have a phone so you can call me?"

"Yes, we both do," Jamie said.

They all climbed in the trailer, and we slid the ramp in and leaned it against the wall.

"Okay, we'll follow you," I said.

We spent the next thirty minutes creeping down the road with the flashers on. Fortunately, it was New Year's Day, and there was almost no traffic. Most of our trip was on dirt roads anyway, but there were a couple of miles on the highway. At last, we arrived at their house.

Honey raised a ruckus in the trailer, and the two horses in the pasture beside us threw an impromptu party. They whinnied, then raced up and down the fence, rearing, bucking and carrying on. Lisa hopped out of the truck yelling at them.

"Hey, you two settle down! Don't get Honey all wound up, or she'll kill herself getting off the trailer!"

"She knows she's home," Erica noted.

The horses ignored her and began play-fighting with one another. They bit each other on the neck and the rump, and kicked out with both rear feet in an impressive display of athleticism.

"The stall is ready to go," Don said. "We just have to get her into it."

He opened the trailer door and I helped him slide the ramp out and set it in place.

"Okay Mom, you're going to have to turn her around," Lisa shouted, trying to make herself heard over the excited neighing. "She can't back down the ramp."

"Okay," Sandy said. "I'm ready when you are."

"Take her to the left," Erica said. "Let's try to go real slow. I'll push her butt over, so she doesn't have to pivot on her front foot so much."

They did a slow-motion spin, which was a little tough with Honey being excited, but they finally got her facing the back of the trailer. We stepped out of the way, and Sandy led her gently down the ramp and into the paddock. Once they got through the gate, they stopped for a rest, then made it around the corner and into a stall in one more move.

"Alright, you all did a great job with that," Erica said. "I think I've found my horse ambulance team."

"Lord, no," Lisa said. "That was way more stress than I can handle on a regular basis."

"Well, you made it look easy," I said. "You all are a great team."

"That's because we have a great leader," Lisa said, giving Erica another hug. "I don't know how we would have gotten through this without you."

I smiled, because I feel that way about Erica too,

regarding just about everything in life. She just has a way of making everything come together, and making people feel confident that it's all going to be fine. She's a real-life Wonder Woman and I have a long list of people who will attest to that!

3

End of the Trail

"Can you tech for me today?"

I was caught off guard by the question, as I sat at my desk in my sweaty workout shorts eating breakfast and watching funny videos on YouTube. I looked at the clock: 7:20 am. Since I do most of my work from home, I was on schedule for that, but if I was leaving in a half hour, I was suddenly way behind schedule.

"Of course, I can," I said. That's the only right answer, after all. "What's up?"

"Katie just texted me and said she's sick." Erica was at the kitchen table, eating a bowl of oatmeal.

"Alright, no worries. I just need to run through the shower quick after I eat."

"Just meet me at the office," Erica said. "That way you can come home when we're done, instead of waiting for me to finish posting everything this afternoon."

Every once in a while, I get to act as the substitute daytime technician, and I really enjoy it most of the time. It doesn't happen often enough for the novelty to wear off. I sped up on eating and checked my calendar to see what I needed to shuffle around with the change of plans. The only big thing I had intended to get done, besides my regular trip to the bank, recycle center, and feed store was inputting the previous month's credit card charges into QuickBooks, and getting that reconciled. Putting it off a day wouldn't change anything.

When I got to the clinic, Liz, who was teching for Dr. Allison, was already stocking Erica's truck for me. She was a stocky, late-thirties, get-things-done kind of gal, with a personality that you couldn't help but like.

"You're a rock star," I said. "What can I do to help?"

"We need clean rags. You can also refill the alcohol-gauze squares and the chlorhexidine gauze."

I'm involved in most of the business aspects of running the clinic, but I don't know very much about this side of things. Liz realizes that, and gives me simple tasks that I can handle without a lot of explanation. This is mainly to expedite the process of getting the trucks stocked and getting to the first appointment on time.

Our first appointment was to check a mare that Erica had inseminated two weeks before. It was a farm that I had been to a few times, so I didn't need her to give me directions to get there, and that made me feel pretty good. As a breeding and training farm, they housed a lot of horses, so there was one big barn, and several smaller barns on the property, surrounded by a complex of paddocks and arenas. I parked us next to the wash rack near the end of the main barn.

"Okay, you grab the ultrasound, the lube, and a sleeve," Erica said. "I'll get the rest of the stuff."

"Deal."

This farm does a lot of breeding, so they have their own stocks, which is very helpful. Stocks are basically just a box that the horse stands in that keeps them from moving around, or kicking you. I set up the ultrasound machine next to the stocks, and one of the farm hands brought the horse over.

Erica spoke to him in Spanish for a minute, presumably asking about how the horse was acting over the last week. She pulled on the shoulder-length plastic sleeve and lubed her hand.

Juan, the farm hand, held the mare's head. I held her tail out of the way, then Erica grabbed the ultrasound wand and slowly inserted her arm into the horse. Due to their size, and the limitations of technology, a lot of things on horses have to be checked by an ultrasound machine from the inside, so you can see what you need to see. Erica shifted a bit, getting the probe into position. A moment later, a large black circle resolved into view on the screen from the white static.

"There it is," Erica said. "Now, as long as there isn't a twin in the other horn, we're good." She spoke rapidly in Spanish for a moment as she repositioned the probe. A moment later, she withdrew her arm and smiled. "All set."

I released her tail, then Juan opened the front of the stocks and led the mare away. Erica stripped off the sleeve while I shut down the ultrasound machine and cleaned the probe in the nearby sink.

"Alright," she said as we climbed back into the truck. "Let's head to High Springs, on the other side of River Rise State Park."

I turned the truck around as Erica checked her phone. We were almost to the gate at the end of the driveway when she changed the plan.

"Never mind that," she said, her fingers flying across the screen on her phone. "We've got an emergency over in Jonesville. Colic."

I turned left instead of right and headed towards Jonesville. She guided me through a series of turns into a rural neighborhood that I'd never seen before.

"I think it's the one with the fish mailbox," she said. "I haven't been here in a while, since Dr. Allison has been seeing them."

I pulled into the driveway. The house was an older plantation-style design, light green with a wrap-around porch on three sides, and several live oak trees shading most of the yard. Behind the house, just visible through the trees and bushes, I could make out a small red barn. We followed the driveway around behind the house and stopped in front of the paddock gate. The barn was at the back of the paddock and was a lean-to with stalls on one side, and storage rooms on the other. There was a woman inside the gate, holding the lead rope of a horse that clearly wasn't trying to go anywhere. We hopped out of the truck.

I went around back and opened the lift gate. Erica stood beside me, waiting for it to raise, when suddenly she clutched my arm and hunched up close to me.

"Oh, shit," she said. The fear in her voice caused me to freeze for a moment. Sensing fear in Erica is sort of like seeing the bomb squad guy running. If she was scared, then I probably needed to panic.

I turned around, not knowing whether to expect an alligator, or an old man with a shotgun, but trying to be ready for either. There, approaching us in full stealth mode like a squad of ninjas, was a small flock of geese. They did seem to be slightly hostile, and I've heard all about how geese are great watchdogs, but I didn't understand why Erica was panicking. She's not afraid of anything, especially in terms of animals.

"I hate geese," she muttered through clenched teeth. "I hate geese, I hate them, I hate them, I hate them."

The geese were getting close. Erica grabbed her stethoscope and fled to the paddock. The geese ignored me and followed her, lining up at the fence as she slammed the gate from the other side. I grabbed the rest of the stuff I expected to need and walked over to the gate. I was feeling a bit cocky for a moment, as the geese seemed to be uninterested in me, but then they changed their mind and charged me. I set my ego down and hurried through the gate, fumbling with the chain in my sudden haste. Once inside, I attempted to restore my dignity. I looked around to make sure I wasn't observed. A pair of eyes peering through the fence rails to my right caught my attention.

The eyes in question were in the next paddock over. They were looking at me between two horizontal slats of fencing, and a set of tall, brown and white ears poked up over the top of the fence. Based on the distance between the eyes and the ears, I determined that it could only be a donkey. I assumed that it was laughing at me, and walked over to the horse, where Erica was taking vitals.

"I need to take a lactate," Erica said. The lactate meter was the one thing I didn't bring. I glanced back at the truck.

"Okay," I said. What else could I say?

I walked back over to the gate and noticed a dog trotting over from the direction of the house. I waited until he was close, and then opened the gate. I was hoping that I could quickly befriend the dog, which I'm pretty good at, and then the geese would see that I was not a threat. Maybe they'd leave me alone. I closed the gate carefully, trying to look confident. The geese immediately came over and gathered behind me as I walked towards the truck. I tried to make eye contact with the dog, but he saw the geese behind me, spun around, and headed back to the house. I was on my own.

I put on my brave face and acted like I wasn't worried about anything. I got to the back of the truck, opened the top center drawer, and pulled out the lactate meter. The geese formed a semi-circle around me, effectively fencing me in against the truck.

"Alright folks," I said, using my deep, I'm-in-charge voice. "I'm going to need you to step back out of the way. This is important medical business."

The geese stared at me, and one of them honked, which made me jump. I silently cursed my jumpiness, and glanced around. Over at the paddock fence, I could see the ears sticking up over the top rail.

"I'm being observed and judged," I announced to the geese, "so I hope you'll understand that I'm not being unnecessarily aggressive here, but I gotta do what I gotta do."

I took a deep breath to steady my nerves and marched through the skirmish line. The goose in front of me scooted to the side, and I walked right by and went back over to the gate. They all followed me, but none of them attacked, for which I was immensely grateful. I was acting tough, but if one of them had bitten me, I probably would have screamed.

Erica pulled some blood, and we ran the lactate test. We watched the screen, and my heart sank when it finally showed the result: 6.4. I looked at Erica, and the glance she gave me confirmed my suspicions. This was not good. The normal range for a healthy horse is anything less than three.

"Is Kathy on her way here?" Erica asked the woman who was holding the horse.

"Yes, she said she was on her way when I talked to her," she replied. "I don't know where she was, though."

"I'm going to go ahead and palpate her and see if I can figure out what's going on," Erica said. "She has a really high lactate, so she's probably going to be a surgical candidate."

"Oh, that's not good," the lady said. "I just clean the barn and feed the animals, so I don't know how she'd want to handle all that."

"No worries," Erica said.

She pulled on the sleeve and lubed it up, while I took the lead rope from the woman.

"We can take it from here, if you have some other stuff you need to do," I said. "Or you can hang out, it's totally up to you."

"Thanks," she replied. "I've got to finish up here so I can get to my other job on time."

She made her way out of the paddock. I noticed that the geese didn't pay any attention to her, and I gave them the hairy eye. Erica palpated the horse, and she had an intense expression on her face.

"What do you think?" I asked.

"Strangulated small intestine," she said grimly. "Either this horse is going to EMC in the next hour for surgery, or we're going to euthanize it. She's in trouble."

She extracted her arm and removed the sleeve.

"Alright, we're going to sedate her and give her some pain meds," she said. "We'll pass a tube and see if we get any reflux. Hopefully, Kathy will be here by then and we can make a plan."

"Do I need to hold her, or will she be alright if I come help you get the stuff?" I asked.

"You stay here and hold her. Don't let her go down. I'll go grab the stuff."

I was torn. On one hand, we were in a very serious situation with a horse that was facing a life or death decision. On the other hand, there was a flock of ninja geese right outside the gate, waiting for Erica, who was deathly afraid of them. The emotional turmoil was nearly too much for me.

Erica opened the gate, paused for a moment, then bolted to the back of the truck. Immediately, the entire flock of geese gave high pursuit, honking wildly, their heads bobbing as they ran towards her. They disappeared behind the truck, and I was stuck in a blind spot, unable to see what was happening.

Suddenly, a large blonde woman came striding into view from the direction of the house. The geese ran over to her, honking and flapping their wings, but I could tell right away that it wasn't an aggressive approach. The woman patted them on the head and shooed them out of her way.

A moment later, she headed for the gate, followed closely by Erica.

"Kathy, this is my husband, Justin," Erica said. "He's filling in for my regular tech today."

"Nice to meet you," I said, shaking her hand. She was almost as tall as me, and probably in her mid-forties. "That's quite a contingent of militant geese you've got there."

"Ah, they're harmless," she said with a laugh. "I raised them all from hatchlings. They think they're dogs. So, what's going on with Peaches?"

Erica found the vein in the horse's neck and gave it two shots. While we waited for the sedation to take effect, she explained the situation.

"So, what we've got is a strangulated small intestine. That means that she's got a lipoma, or a fatty tumor, and those usually hang off the abdomen on a tissue, like a string. Most horses get these as they age, and sometimes, like this, the tumor gets wrapped around the small intestine. Now it's cutting off circulation. We see this in older horses, and she palpated like a classic strangulation."

"Oh, no," said Kathy. "Is it fixable?"

"A lot of them do make it through surgery," Erica said. "Not all of them make it long-term post-surgery, though. They tend to founder a week or two after surgery. I'd say about twenty percent of them make a decent recovery."

"Those aren't good odds," Kathy said. I watched the lines on her face deepen as the color drained away. When she spoke again, there was a tremor in her voice. "How much does the surgery cost?"

"If we sent her to EMC, it would start around eight thousand," Erica said. "If we sent her to the University, a little more than that."

Kathy's face fell. She leaned against Peaches and wrapped her arms around her neck. "Oh, my baby girl, don't do this." Her voice was muffled by the horse's fur, but her grief was radiating off her in waves. There was a burning sensation in my nose, and I knew the tears wouldn't be far behind it. Peaches stood still with her head hanging down near her knees.

"She's twenty-nine years old," Kathy said. She pulled a crumpled Kleenex from her pocked and blew her nose. Tears were running down her cheek as she turned towards us. "I'm not going to put her through all that with an eighty percent chance that she's going to die, anyway."

"I've got her sedated, and we're going to pass a tube and see if she's got any reflux," Erica said. "We're trying to make her as comfortable as we can. If you want to call anyone, or take some time, by all means do so. We don't have to do anything right this second."

"Okay, let me call my husband and the kids," Kathy said. Her chest heaved as she fumbled for her phone, and she began crying. "I'm not ready for this. My kids grew up riding Peaches. She was the one they both learned to ride on. Hell, I've had her since I was in college." She scrubbed her nose with the Kleenex.

"It's the hardest thing in the world with these old guys," Erica said. "I've been through it with two of mine, so I know. There isn't anything you can do to make it hurt any less when you've loved them for that long."

"I know it," Kathy said. "You try to be ready for this day to come, but I don't think you can." She blew her nose again and jammed the tissue back in her pocket with a sigh.

"Okay, let me call everyone." She leaned over and gave the horse another hug, and then turned away with her phone.

"Let's pass the tube," Erica said.

Peaches was not happy about the tube, despite being sedated and having pain medication. I did my best to hold her head still. I scratched her forehead and her ears, and whispered soothing sounds to try to calm her down as Erica passed the tube up her nose and into her stomach. Horses are physically incapable of vomiting, and since we knew her intestines were blocked, our goal with the tube was to see if she had a lot of water in her stomach and remove whatever we could. Just because she can't throw up doesn't mean she doesn't need to.

"Okay," Erica said. "Let's pump a bit of water into her."

I handed the lead rope to her and squatted down by the bucket. By pumping a bit of water into her, we were effectively creating a siphon with which we could pull off any fluids that were built up in her stomach. I attached the hose to the pump and pumped the handle six times. Erica nodded at me.

As soon as I pulled the hose off the pump, the water began flowing back out. We could see the green fluid filling the clear hose, which was partially-digested hay and grass mixed in with the water she had been drinking. I guessed that we pulled around a gallon of water out of her before the flow slowed to a trickle, and then stopped.

"Well, that ought to make her feel better," I said. The smell was nauseating, and I leaned away from the puddle on the ground.

Erica nodded, removing the tube. "It'll help, but she's hurting in a way we can't fix."

I stood up and gathered all the things we had brought out to the paddock.

"You want to get everything ready, and be staged over at the truck?" I asked quietly.

"We can put all this away, if you want to, but let's wait on the rest of it. They might change their mind and send her to surgery. It's happened before."

That made sense to me. This was an emotionally charged situation, and us humans aren't always at our best in these moments. I carried everything over to the gate, wary of the geese, but with Kathy here, they seemed to have lost interest in chasing me. That was a relief.

When I got back to the paddock, Erica and Kathy were talking. A moment later a car pulled up beside the vet truck.

"That's my daughter, and my son is on the way," Kathy said. "We're going to let everyone say goodbye to Peaches. My husband can't get away from work." She paused for a moment. "If you don't mind, I'd like to bury her right there in the paddock under the live oak. It's her favorite place to hang out."

I nodded. As her daughter came running up, Erica and I made our way to the back of the truck to give them their privacy. Within minutes, a second car pulled up, and a young man in his early twenties got out and joined them.

"They must have been close by," I said.

"They live in one of those big houses right down the street," Erica explained. "This place was Kathy's mother's house, and they keep all the farm stuff here, but they live in their own house. The kids are both in college."

"Ahh," I said. "Well, it's fortunate that they weren't in class at the moment."

After about ten minutes, Kathy stepped back and waved us over, meeting us at the gate.

"Okay," she said. "I don't want her to suffer any longer. Let's get it over with."

"Alright," Erica said. "Give me just a minute to get everything ready."

We went to the back of the truck, and Erica pulled two large syringes of euthanasia solution, and a smaller syringe of a nerve block, while I put a few catheters and the clippers in the tray. Erica went over the procedure with me quickly, just as a refresher. One of the down sides of being the night and weekend emergency tech is that I have attended a fair number of end-of-life events for horses.

"You're going to hold the lead rope," she said. "I'll shave a spot on her neck and hand you the clippers. I'll block the area so she doesn't feel anything, then hand you the needle. I'll confirm with Kathy. I'll insert the catheter and then ask everyone to step back. You give me the two syringes, which I put in my pocket. When everyone is back, I'll administer both syringes as fast as I can, toss them away, and then I'll take the lead rope. You get back quick. I'll guide her down as best as I can. You find the syringes and the family comes up. Got it?"

"Got it."

We walked back over to Peaches and the family, stopping a few feet away. They were all three crying and laughing, while telling each other stories about various moments with the horse. We gave them all the time they wanted. At last, Kathy gave Peaches a big hug, and stepped back.

"Alright," she said. "I don't want her to suffer any longer, and the pain meds are going to wear off if we keep on. You kids give her a hug, and let's let her go to heaven."

Erica waited until all the hugs were done, and then stepped forward.

"Ok," she said. "I'm going to inject her and she's going to go down fast, within a few seconds. You all are welcome to be here for it if that's what you want, or you can go inside, if you'd rather not see it. I'll warn you, there's no pretty way to do this: she's going to fall. The good news is that she won't feel it."

"I'm going inside," Kathy's daughter said. "I can't watch it."

"Me too," her son said. "I'd rather not have that in my head."

"I totally understand," Erica said.

"I'm going to stay," Kathy said. "I've been through everything in her life, and I'm not going to make her do this without me." Her jaw clinched in grim determination and a spot of red bloomed on her cheeks, but her sagging shoulders showed the tremendous emotional weight that she carried.

The kids went inside, and Erica quickly shaved a spot on the horse's neck over the vein. I held on to the lead rope with one hand, and took the clippers from her with the other hand, setting them in the tray at my feet. The block went next, and then the catheter. Kathy scratched Peaches on the forehead one more time, kissed her on the nose, then stepped back.

"Are you ready?" Erica asked.

Kathy nodded, tears streaming down her face.

I slid the tray back with my foot and readied myself. This is a pretty tough thing, no matter how many times you do it. Erica put the first syringe in the catheter and plunged it down as fast as she could, tossed it over her shoulder, and jammed the second syringe in and emptied it equally fast. Peaches was already going. I stepped backed, giving Erica room to step around in front of her, and as soon as she had the halter, I snatched up the tray and stepped away.

Peaches swayed back, then forward. She snorted once, then held her breath. Her eyes locked on to Erica, and she blew out the lungful of air in a wheezing cough. Her legs buckled a moment later and she collapsed. With a hand on each side of the halter, Erica shoved Peaches to one side as she fell, and lifted her head at the last moment so that it didn't hit the ground too hard.

Kathy's shoulders shook as grief wracked her body. She let out a cry that held so much pain that I couldn't stop the tears that began streaming down my cheeks. I thought about the way I felt when I had sent my dog, Angus, to heaven. It seemed like a big giant hole had been ripped open in my gut that day, and I knew Kathy felt that way now. Erica confirmed that there were no vitals or pupil reaction, and nodded to Kathy.

"She's gone," Erica said softly. "You gave her a pretty great life, and that's better than a lot of horses get."

Kathy nodded slowly. She took a shuddering step forward and melted into a heap on the ground beside Peaches. She cried hard for a few minutes, rubbing her neck and absently running her fingers through Peaches' mane. I wiped my eyes with my shirt sleeve, wishing that I had brought a paper towel from the truck to blow my nose with. Erica grabbed my hand and squeezed it for a minute. I glanced over, and saw that her eyes were shining, too.

"I'd like to keep a bit of her tail hair," Kathy said, blowing her nose again, and trying to get herself together. "I want to find that place that makes memorial jewelry out of manes and tails." She glanced up at Erica. "Do you know what I'm talking about? The place that makes woven bracelets and earrings?"

"Yep, I sure do," Erica said, pulling out her scissors and a plastic baggie. "I actually know of a couple of different places that do that. Do you want to cut it, or would you like me to?"

"I will," said Kathy.

I removed the catheter from Peaches' neck, collected the syringes, and took the tray back to the truck to put everything away. Erica talked with Kathy a few more minutes, and then came over. I had the computer set up for her, and she quickly entered everything. Kathy came over to the truck just as she was finishing up.

"Erica, can I just give you a credit card now?" she asked.

"Sure, however you want to handle it," Erica said. "If you don't want to deal with that right this minute, I can email it to you for later."

"No, no, I don't want to make you wait. You've been fantastic to us for a lot of years, and I'd rather just take care of it right now."

"Okay," said Erica. She ran the card and handed it back.

"You know, Dr. Allison has been coming out here lately," Kathy said. "We just love her to pieces. I think you found yourself a top-notch associate."

"Thank you! We think an awful lot of her, too," Erica said. "The really good ones are so hard to find."

"Thank you again for doing this," Kathy said. "You've always been the most wonderful person, and I'm glad you were here to get us through it."

I hear this from people a lot. Many of them take me aside and tell me what a great woman I married. I know she's incredible, but it really inspires me to see the positive impact she has on all the people in her life. I was thinking about that as we drove away, and about how you never know where the day is going to take you when you wake up in the morning. I never know, anyway.

The emergency had set us back a bit on our schedule, so Erica called the office to have them let the rest of our appointments know that we were running late. I realized that this was a harsh reality of being a veterinarian. You have to be able to deal with everything that had just happened, and then arrive at your next appointment with a cheerful smile and make that person and their horse the center of your universe. That's something that Erica is really good at, but I also gained a new appreciation for her need to come home and vent a lot of sadness or pain to me sometimes. The emotions are real, and you've got to do something with them, so they don't consume you.

We finished out the scheduled appointments for the day, which consisted of a dental float, a bunch of vaccines, and a pre-purchase exam. I was worn out when we got back to the clinic, but there was still enough time to make it to the bank and the feed store, so I hopped in my truck and went. I did a lot of thinking about things as I drove. It seemed profound to me in that moment that for most of us, life goes on, but for Peaches, it was the end of the trail. For Kathy and her family, it was the end of an era. For me, it was a reality check about life, death, the impermanence of things, and how things change whether we want them to or not. I was glad that Peaches had someone to cry for her. Not everyone does.

4

Living in the Animal House

One of the many advantages to working from home is that I don't have to be at the office at a certain time anymore. With zero travel time, I can take a shower, shave, and walk out to the living room to my desk, and I'm at work. The ambiance is great, as we live out in the country. We live on twenty acres, five of which are woods, and the rest of which are pastures, except where the barn and buildings are. One side is bordered by a state park, which is all forest on our side. The side adjoining that one is a twenty-acre block of woods that is undeveloped and separates us from our neighbor with the goats.

The layout is pretty simple. The primary structure is an eight-stall barn, with a tiny two-bedroom apartment on top of it where we live. There is a mother-in-law suite across the driveway, and that's where my mother-in-law lives when she's in town. She's a business consultant and spends a lot of time on the road. The two dogs are actually hers, although they live here full time instead of travelling with her.

One of the big advantages of working from home is the co-workers. We have five cats and two dogs who are coming and going on their mysterious errands all day, and five horses downstairs munching on hay and snoozing in their stalls all day, and another horse and a donkey out in the field munching on grass all day.

One of the big disadvantages of working from home is the co-workers. We have five cats, two of which are ready and willing to stand on the keyboard when you are trying to type, dying to be pet when you are focused on something important, and any of them could bring a dragonfly in from outside and release it, at which point all the cats and dogs join in the game of *Catch the dragonfly*. We also have five horses downstairs, any one of which might get a sudden itch and need to scratch their neck on the stall door for five minutes, which creates a tremendous racket. Or, one might decide that three pm is close enough to supper time, and start kicking their stall door, which makes it sound like the whole house and barn are coming down.

One day, in the first few months after I moved in, the madness started before I even got to work (the living room). Erica was already gone for the day, and I was standing in the bathroom, shaving. I hadn't been in the shower yet, as that was my next planned activity after shaving. So, I stood there, naked and with shaving cream all over my face and neck, not a care in the world, when I heard the cat on the end of the bathroom counter start rumbling out this very peculiar meow/snarl. (I should mention that I have since learned that this is an early warning signal that things are about to get exciting, and probably not in a good way). Not realizing what was happening, I stuck my head out in the hallway just in time to see a bird come flying up the hall, bouncing off the walls. It brushed my face with just enough contact to allow it to fling shaving cream everywhere. It was hotly pursued by three cats and a Jack Russell terrier, and a moment later by a naked man with shaving cream and a look of horror on his face, razor still in his hand.

The bird flew into the bedroom. On one hand, this was good, because we have French doors in the bedroom that open up onto the front porch. On the other hand, it was bad, because there were two cats on the outside of those doors, watching us with great intensity. While I was registering all this, the bird made its way around the room and back into the hall, somehow avoiding the ceiling fan. I decided to go ahead and open the French doors, in the event that I managed to get the bird back in here. I figured the cats on the outside would come through the cat door in the kitchen and join in the fray anyway. I sprinted to the kitchen to open the other door, and came around the corner just as Pesca leaped off the cat tower to try to grab the bird out of the air. He missed the bird, but hit me right in the face. Undeterred, he hit the ground running, leaving shaving cream footprints everywhere.

The bird had nowhere to go in the kitchen, as I hadn't managed to get that door open yet, so it turned around and shot back down the hall. I opened the door and turned to follow them down the hall. My front foot slipped on the shaving cream where Pesca had landed, and I almost did the splits. I managed to catch myself with the refrigerator door, and I hobbled down the hall. Rachel, the pit bull, heard the ruckus from outside and came through the front door at two hundred miles an hour. She passed me in the hall, bouncing off my knee and stepping on my foot on her way by. I somehow managed to avoid falling, but by the time I made it to the bedroom, the cats and dogs were all out on the porch, and the bird was nowhere to be seen.

"Who brought that bird in the house?" I demanded. No one said anything. The dogs crowded around my feet looking for some attention, but I was in no mood for that.

"Let me tell you how this is going to work," I said, pointing at the cats with the razor to emphasize my point. "There are twenty acres out here for you to play your little games on. Twenty acres! Most cats don't even have two acres, much less twenty. Now, all you have do to stay out of trouble is play outside, and don't bring anything inside that's alive. Or dead, for that matter. Understood?"

No one listens to a naked man on a front porch with shaving cream smeared all over him, especially when he's lecturing with a razor for a stylus. The cats yawned and wandered off. The dogs pretended to care what I was talking about, but it was only a ruse to get petted. I limped back inside to try to put the house back in order.

...

The body count inside the house at any given moment was a pretty good sign that my rules didn't mean much to the cats.

There's a game called *Grab the Grasshopper* that the cats love to play. One cat will catch a grasshopper out in the yard and bring it inside. At this point the other cats see what's happening, and they begin making that noise I was telling you about. The cat with the grasshopper then rips off one of the grasshopper's back legs and lets it go. The poor grasshopper, with only one propulsion leg, flies sideways, bouncing off the walls, furniture, et cetera as the cats all run around and try to catch him in the air. This involves a lot of jumping, and strategic placing of one's self, such as on the arm of the couch so you can make a lateral grab if it comes by, or perhaps on the lap of the guy at the desk, so that you can sink all your claws into his leg as you launch yourself into the air.

There is a similar game called *Catch the Dragonfly*. In this game, the unfortunate dragonfly loses a wing instead of a leg, but the rest of the game is the same. The other game in that series is called *Lizard*, and that's the one that leaves the goriest mess. I have determined that if you are a bad person in life, you get reincarnated as a grasshopper, dragonfly, or a lizard, and you are born at my house. There's a lot of torture involved.

It's great fun to sit on the rocking chair on the porch and eat lunch when the cats are trying to catch grasshoppers and dragonflies out in the pastures. Since the porch is on the second floor, it's the best place to watch the action. It usually starts with a lengthy stalk, as the cat belly-creeps forward. Suddenly, they spring into the air, sometimes four or five feet, twisting and reaching, claws extended, body turning to follow the trajectory of the panicking target. I haven't determined the average number of failed attempts per catch, but it's probably a fairly high number.

...

I really do love working from home. I was trying to reconcile the bank statement one day when my mother-in-law, Elise, came upstairs.

"I'm going to ride Gigi for a bit," she said. "If you don't hear from me in an hour, call an ambulance."

"Okay," I said. "Have a good time."

I returned to my piles of receipts, statement sheets and computer screens, trying not to lose track of where I was at. Sometime later, and I'm not sure if it was two minutes or ten minutes, I saw a blur of movement out the window behind my desk. I stood up so I could see over my monitor, and there it was again, a horse running across the yard. Since there was no saddle on it, I could at least feel fairly certain that Elise hadn't fallen off. I slipped on some shoes and hustled downstairs. Elise was walking around the back corner of the barn as I turned down the center aisle, and I could hear her through the open barn windows.

"Goddammit Gigi, get over here," she shouted. Her head bobbed past a window.

Gigi went galloping down the other side of the barn. I grabbed a halter off the rack and jogged out to help catch her. We finally cornered her down by the front pastures. Gigi was breathing hard and sweating, as was Elise. I tried very hard not to laugh, lest I pour gas on the fire.

"Well," I ventured, "at least she's warmed up now."

"She's not as warm as she's going to be," Elise replied in a menacing tone, but she quickly brightened. "Sometimes I forget how slick she is with getting a halter off. I walked her out of the stall, and I turned left, and she turned right, and just like that, she was loose." She laughed. "I guess that means I've been slacking. I need to get on her more often."

They managed to get through their ride without any more excitement, and I managed to get the bank statement reconciled to Quickbooks. Seriously though, can you ask for a better distraction from work? This kind of thing never happened at my old office job.

The big brown blur, which is what I call it when a horse goes zipping by my window, has happened several other times. We rotate pastures with the horses, so that the grass can get a break and grow back every few weeks. Sometimes this can work out so that a horse is out front all by itself for a bit, and everyone else is in the back pastures. Each horse has a pasture buddy, of course, but if their pasture buddy is about to go for a ride, they might go out alone.

This happened to Sydney a while back. Horses are wired funny. It's something that you just have to see to believe, but this is how it appears to work: if a horse is in a place where it cannot see another horse, it will immediately come to the conclusion that it is the only horse left on the planet. Yes, you might have thought that the alien abduction crowd was all people, but I'm here to tell you that it's mostly horses. Horses, and maybe a few guys in New Mexico.

Anyway, Bridget, who is the college kid that takes care of the barn for us in the evenings, was putting the horses out one night. It was a pasture rotate day. Angie, who was Sydney's pasture buddy, stayed in the barn. Sydney came to the [obvious] conclusion that everyone else had been abducted by aliens, so she came racing up and jumped the gate. It's a pretty impressive jump because the ground is low at the front of the gate from all the foot traffic. The top of the gate is easily five feet high, maybe a bit more. She went flying by my window, neighing and whinnying, and ran to the back pastures where the other horses were.

Bridget came out of the barn where she had been cleaning stalls. Her long blonde hair was in a ponytail that was poking out the back of a John Deere cap, and her jeans were tucked into her cowboy boots, as they usually were.

"What was that all about?" she asked, glancing up. I was on the porch at this point, watching the excitement.

"Aliens," I replied.

She nodded solemnly, then grabbed a halter and walked out to get Sydney. I went back inside once Bridget had a hold of her. I had just figured out where I left off when Sydney came racing by again, screaming her fool head off all the way to the back field.

"I didn't even get back to the barn this time," Bridget said. "She jumped the gate like it was nothing. You all need to get her back jumping at horse shows."

"I guess so," I replied. "She's got plenty of energy for it."

"You want me to just keep her in the barn until Angie's ready to go out?"

"Yeah, I don't think we have a lot of choice," I said. "She's either going to be there, or out back."

It's a good lesson to remember: a horse is going to do what the horse wants to do. If they're doing what you want them to do, it's because they feel like it, not because they have to.

· · ·

Another benefit of working from home is break time. When I need to get up and walk around, or get away from the computer for a while and clear my head, I'm not confined to an office building. One of my hobbies is painting, and it's pretty cool to be able to hang up the phone from yet another hostile phone call with AT&T, turn around, pick up a brush, and start working on my current art project.

Sometimes painting in the living room can get challenging. There are a lot of tails that stick straight up in the air as the bodies under them stroll around in all the most inopportune places and times.

Once, while I was working on a big painting of a Mahi Mahi, my phone rang on the desk behind me. I had just loaded the brush with green paint, and I turned around to glance at the phone to see who was calling.

As I made eye contact with the phone, I felt the familiar brush on my leg of a cat coming through. A nanosecond later, I felt pressure on the paintbrush. I spun back around just in time to see Pesca, who is a white cat, wander off with a neon green stripe on his tail. Of course, being a cat, he walked straight over to the couch and rubbed against it, leaving a streak of green paint, then headed down the hall.

Running after a cat is a terrible plan if you actually want to catch one, but I was desperate to get him before he jumped up on the bed, which is covered in a white blanket. Fortunately, he thought we were playing, so he turned through the bathroom, shot back out to the kitchen, and headed out the cat door, upon which he left another green smear. On the down side, he disappeared outside, and the paint on his tail was dry before I saw him again. On the upside, the damage inside the house was minimal, so I considered the whole thing a success.

...

It's interesting to see how different the cats are from one another. Pesca and Ari, who are brothers and under three years old, are very similar. They love to play, they have a lot of personality, they like a lot of affection, and they want to be in the middle of everything. They are the ones who usually catch the grasshopper, or the dragonfly, or the lizard. They love to wrestle. Interestingly, Ari loves to chase the red dot of the laser pointer, but Pesca couldn't care less about it.

Oswald is a Maine Coon, and he mostly just eats, sleeps and pukes up hairballs. Occasionally he will get a wild hair and go outside and catch a lizard to play with, but mostly he likes basking and napping. He waddles along at the back of the pack when playing Grasshopper, and doesn't usually try too hard, but he likes the excitement of it all.

Ofeibea is very aloof, hostile, and stand-offish. Apparently, she didn't used to be like that, but when Ari and Pesca showed up, they had a falling out which has lasted to this day, and now she is a bitter, angry cat. She likes climbing trees and beating up Pesca when he tries to stalk her. She fights for real. She often stays outside at night, despite the fact that this is a serious violation of The Rules.

Alice is the true oddball of the bunch. She has an anxiety disorder that doesn't allow her to be seen or touched by anyone. This is complicated by the fact that she was wired to be a lap cat, and she wants very much to be loved and petted, but she just can't quite do it. Once a month or so, she will have a really good day where she manages to stand still as you walk by, instead of fleeing for the safety of the nearest piece of furniture. You might even be able to pet her for just a moment. When this happens, you can't look directly at her, and you can't take it personally when she runs away after a few seconds. It's hard to be Alice.

I guess what it all comes down to is that this is a great place to live and work, or be a cat, or a dog, or a horse. Maybe not such a great place to be a grasshopper, a dragonfly, or a lizard, but for everybody else, it's pretty awesome.

5

Three Ring Circus

"So, you want to go to work with me tomorrow?" Erica asked me one night, during dinner.

"Sure, does your tech need a day off?" I asked.

"No, she'll be there," Erica said. "I don't need you to work, I just thought you might want to tag along."

I thought about that for a moment. Erica doesn't ever ask me to tag along, so this must be some exceptional situation. "So, what's happening?" I asked.

Erica broke into a grin, unable to hide her giddy excitement any longer. "We're going to see the circus people!"

Dave and Pam are animal trainers, and they spend most of the year on the road with a circus. I had heard great stories about them and their animals, and I wasn't about to miss a chance to go see them while they were in town.

"They're getting ready to head out on the new season," Erica continued. "We're going to give them their annual check-up, vaccines, pull blood for Coggins tests, and all that stuff to get them ready to go."

The next day we headed out to Pam's house first thing in the morning. Pam met us at the gate of an ordinary-looking farm with a massive fence around it. It was at least ten feet tall, with telephone poles for fence posts holding up heavy-gage hog wire.

"Hey guys," she called. "Park right over there, we've got everybody more or less ready."

Pam was very charismatic and full of energy, and I liked her immediately. She was tall, slim, and dark-haired, and she walked fast. I guessed her age at around fifty, but it was hard to tell. She closed the gate behind us and walked up just as we got out.

"Pam, this is Justin, my husband," Erica said.

"Hi Pam, I've heard wonderful things about you," I said with a grin. "Thanks for letting me come along."

Pam ignored my proffered hand and gave me a hug. "If Erica likes you enough to marry you, then you're family to me," she said, her face lighting up in a grin. "Welcome to the nuthouse."

Erica and her tech, Amber, were preparing the vaccines, so I took the opportunity to look around. Off to my right, I could see two camels standing in the trees. To the left of them, a goat was standing on the roof of a big red doghouse, which I assumed was now a goat house. There was a white tractor-trailer with a giant ramp coming out of the side of it.

Beyond that was a single-story red barn with a llama poking his head around the corner of it, and a white donkey behind the llama. A large, bearded man came out of the barn. He was leading something that wasn't sure it wanted to come out. He turned back towards the barn and clucked a few times, and suddenly a zebra appeared.

"Dave's loading the zebras in the chute now," Pam said. "We'll do them first, if that's alright."

"Yep, perfect," Erica said. "Give me just a second to get everything together."

"Why the chute?" I asked. "Aren't they just getting a couple of shots?"

Pam laughed, stuck her arm through mine, and walked me over towards the barn. "Zebras are wild animals, even with the best of training," she explained. "They're not a domesticated species. When someone pokes them with a needle, they assume you want to fight to the death, and they try to kill you. So, just to keep Erica safe, we put them in the chute. It keeps us safe, too."

"That totally makes sense," I said.

We walked past a pen full of quacking ducks. "Those are the Julias," Pam said. "They're Indian Running Ducks. That one at the water bowl is Zombie Julia. She was in a coma for a while last year, and it took us forever to nurse her back to health."

"I've heard of her," I said, excited to actually see the infamous duck. "Erica did a bunch of research on ducks last year, trying to figure out what was going on with her."

"Yep, that's the one," Pam said. We stopped to watch the ducks for a moment. "We would never be able to do this stuff without Erica. She has been such an amazing vet. I just love her to death."

"Me, too," I laughed. "She's the most amazing person I've ever met."

"I'm serious," Pam said. "If somebody gets sick while we're on the road, she finds us the right vet to see wherever we are, gets me directions and phone numbers, explains all the things I need to know, you name it. She's also talked us through a lot of things over the phone that we were able to treat ourselves, like when Hannah came down with White Line Disease." She nodded towards the barn. "Hannah Banana is the donkey."

I could tell she felt very strongly about Erica, and that really made me proud. I watched the ducks a moment longer. They were very tall, and stood almost straight up, more like a penguin stance than a Mallard duck stance. The five of them walked in a single-file line around the pen, their heads bobbing forward and back with each step. It was impossible not to laugh, just watching them.

"Wait until you see them jump through the hula hoop," Pam said. "It's a riot."

Erica and Amber caught up with us, and we all walked over to the chute, where Dave was attempting to coax the zebra into the headstall. Pam detached her arm from mine and went over to help.

"Hang back for a second," she said over her shoulder.

We watched as they clucked and cooed and coaxed with treats, and at last the zebra stuck her head through the end. Dave fussed over her, giving her pats and praise.

"You can't force them," he explained as he gave her another treat. "They're stronger than superman when they don't want to do something."

Erica and Amber quickly went to work, not wanting to keep the zebra in the chute any longer than necessary.

"This is Lady Gaga, right?" Amber asked.

"Right," said Dave. "Wama hates going first on anything except supper."

Erica listened to her heart, lungs, and gut sounds, looking her over and feeling various things. Satisfied with her exam, she quickly administered the vaccines and pulled a small vial of blood.

"She's in great shape," Erica announced, stepping back. "Your feeding plan for last year was spot on. She's lost a lot of that extra weight." She pulled out her pocket notebook and wrote down the vitals as Dave carefully eased her out of the chute and back towards the barn.

"Do you want to do the ducks while he's getting Wama out here?" Pam asked.

"Sure, we can do that," Erica replied, putting her notebook away.

The duck exam went quickly, and Dave managed to get the second zebra in the chute without any trouble. When Erica was finished with her, we headed over to the goat, who was still standing on his roof.

"Dillon Dillon," Pam called, snapping her fingers. "You've got company!" Dillon Dillon immediately jumped off his roof and ran away from us.

"Yeah, he remembers me," Erica said with a chuckle. We fanned out and semi-surrounded him.

"Now, come on Dillon Dillon," Pam admonished him. "Is that how a gentleman behaves? Stand."

Dillon Dillon stood still but regarded us with distrust. Pam managed to get a hold of his collar, and sat down beside him, pulling him onto her lap and wrapping him in a bear hug.

"Okay Justin, reach in my hip pouch and get a handful of treats," she directed me. "I'll hold him, you stuff food in his mouth a little piece at a time to distract him, and they can do what they've got to do."

I could tell this was a system that had been used before. I got a handful of pellets and sat down beside her.

"Hiya, Dillon Dillon," I said.

"Baaaaaaaa," he replied. I couldn't tell if it was a positive statement or not.

I handed him a few pieces of food as Erica quickly went to work on him. His lips were impressively nimble as he pulled each pellet from my hand. I scratched under his chin and behind his ears, which he seemed to appreciate.

"Don't feed him all the food too fast," Pam warned. "He'll clean you out if you let him. He's a pro when it comes to suckering people for treats. It's part of what he does for a living."

Dillon Dillon didn't seem to be offended by this. He stretched his head forward, plying my hand for more treats.

"All done," Erica announced. I ruffled his mane one more time as Pam turned him loose. He immediately ran over and jumped back onto the roof of his house.

Next, we went to the camels. Dave was waiting with them.

"This one is Khan," he said. "Do you want them standing, or kneeling first?"

"Standing is fine," Erica said. "Let me just look him over quick, and then we'll get him kushed for his shots."

I watched in fascination as Erica performed the physical

exam. The camel towered over her, and stood still with his long neck twisted around, watching her as she listened to his various sounds. She scratched his ears as she walked around the other side, and he stopped watching her, shifting his attention instead to a leafy branch overhead. He pulled one of the leaves off and chewed on it experimentally. Apparently, it didn't taste very good. He spit it out.

"Okay," Erica said at last. "We can kush him."

Dave tapped Khan on the knee with a stick and said something, and Khan began kneeling down with a sigh. It was like watching a ship sink in the ocean. When he was settled, Dave held the halter, and Erica gave him the vaccines and pulled blood. Khan seemed to be bored with the whole operation.

The second camel was Sheba, and she was the same as Khan: laid back and uninterested in us. Dave murmured things to her, gave her a treat when it was over, and then we all made our way over to the tractor-trailer.

Pam gave a whistle that stunned my eardrums. "Zoey! Busker! Come on, everybody out! Bongo, let's go," she called.

A sudden flurry of activity could be heard in the trailer, and five dogs appeared, racing down the ramp, led by a Chihuahua.

"Ike!" Pam cried, clapping her hands. "Ike, up!" Ike, the Chihuahua, leaped from the ramp to her knee. I laughed at myself, as I was totally expecting Ike to somehow shoot up into her arms. She bent down and picked him up.

"Okay, first victim is Ike," she announced, handing him to Amber.

The rest of the dogs sat in a row at the base of the ramp. It was a motley collection of dogs.

"These are all rescues," Pam said. "The Jack Russell is Busker, the other terrier is Zoey, the Blue Heeler mix with the Dalmatian coloring is Dingo, and this here is Bongo," she said, squatting down by the one on the end. "God knows what he is. He's got the body of a basset hound, and the fur and ears of a border collie." She scratched his ears affectionately.

"I didn't know you could train a Chihuahua," I said. "What does he do?

"Oh, you can train anything," Pam said. "It just takes time and a commitment to working with them every day. Ike does several jumping tricks, runs on top of the barrel, rides the horse, all kinds of stuff."

"Wow," I said. "That's pretty impressive."

"Once we get everybody done, we'll run through the act," Pam said. "It'll be a good rehearsal for us in front of an audience, and you can see what these guys are all about."

"That's my favorite part," said Erica. "We get to see the show every year before anybody else." She sat Ike back down on the ramp. "Who's next?"

"Busker, up," Pam said, pointing at her chest. Busker leaped into her arms, excited to have his turn.

"I thought that's what Ike was going to do," I admitted. "I got all wrapped up in the moment."

"That's exactly what you were supposed to think," Pam laughed. "That means we did a good job selling you on it."

When the dogs were all done, Erica and Amber went back to the truck to draw up the rest of the vaccines and put the blood in the cooler, as the vials were starting to overflow the tray. When they were ready, we went over by the barn.

"Tony, come see Erica," Pam called. The llama stuck

his head around the corner, just as he did earlier. His neck seemed to be about a mile long.

"This is Tony," Pam said. "The theme this year is 'The Wild, Wild West' so I made him a cowboy outfit. He's going to be Tony Llama."

We all laughed. Sensing that the attention was on him, Tony strutted out and bleated a few times. We made our way through the gate, and Pam slipped a halter on Tony.

His hair was very long, and he was mostly white, with a few brown splotches. I gave him a pat on the neck and was surprised at how soft he was.

"Tony is our front man," Pam explained. "He loves wearing costumes and posing for pictures, and he's great with kids. Last year he was Uncle Sam."

"I saw him on Facebook," said Amber. "Someone had tagged you, and it was Tony in the Uncle Sam outfit with like ten kids."

"Yep, that sounds about right," Pam said. "He's a total ham."

Suddenly I felt lips on my hand. I jumped and spun around to see what was trying to eat me. The white donkey stood there, and stretched her head out to sniff my hand again.

"Ah, I bet she smells the treats I was feeding the goat," I said with a chuckle.

"That's Hannah," Erica said. "She's coming to stay with us this year while they go on the road."

"Sweet!" I said. "Pet finally gets a friend." I gave Hannah a scratch behind her giant ears, and showed her my empty palm on the hand she was so interested in. "Do you do any tricks?" I asked hopefully.

"She did a number act with Dave last year," Pam said.

"They had a bunch of boards with zero through nine painted on them. Dave would ask her what two plus three was, and she would go pick up the five. He'd ask her what twelve minus eight was, and she'd pick up the four. He'd ask her what the IQ of the guy in the green t-shirt was, and she'd pick up the two. She used to smile on command, but she won't hardly do that one anymore."

"That's amazing," I said. "How do you teach her math?"

"Oh, it's a hand command," Pam explained. "If Dave holds up one finger, she goes to a certain board, if he holds up three fingers, she goes to another one. They don't actually use all ten boards, but you wouldn't ever realize that watching the act."

"So, the verbal stuff is for the audience, and what he's doing with her is all hand gestures. That's brilliant!"

Pam gave me a wink. "That's show business."

Two miniature horses in an adjoining pen were next on the list, and the mule beyond them was last. He was eye-catching, to say the least. He was white, and covered in black spots, like a Dalmatian. As soon as we got near, the mule crossed his front legs, dropped his head, and swayed back and forth.

"Whoa," I said. "Is he alright?" Everyone laughed, and I guessed that I was missing something.

"This is Rowdy," Erica explained. "He does a drunk mule act. He does it every time someone walks by, hoping for a treat."

I had to admit it was a pretty convincing act. With his bizarre colorings, large ears, and the drunk act, you couldn't help but pay attention to him.

"He picks up a whiskey bottle and chugs it down at the beginning of the act," Pam said. "But if he doesn't have the prop, he goes on with the act anyway. He's a real pro." She patted his neck. "He's not going with us this year, either. He's getting older, and I think he needs to hang out in a pasture for a season and relax; give the body a break."

Once he had his shots, Pam pointed towards the ring behind the trailer. "You go get your stuff put away, and we'll meet you over there. We won't do the whole show, but I'll run through the smaller animals."

Ten minutes later, we gathered on the edge of the ring. The two miniature horses stood beside the gate. One had a saddle on, with a pole-mounted dummy dressed as a cowboy fixed to the saddle. His left hand was raised up in a wave, and his right was on the saddle horn. The other horse had a thick pad strapped on like a saddle. Pam pulled out her phone, fiddled with it a moment, and suddenly a honky-tonk piano began playing saloon music over the speakers beside the gate.

Pam gave another ear-piercing whistle, and the Julia's came running into the ring. They were in a single file line, then began circling the perimeter, quacking and head-bobbing as they waddled. I was so enthralled in the amusement of the moment it didn't even occur to me to pull out my phone and video any of it. Pam stepped into the ring with a hula hoop. She held it out in front of her about six inches off the ground, and as the line of ducks came around, they hopped through it, one by one, then exited the ring. We all laughed and clapped.

Another whistle brought the dogs in at a run. They raced over, hopped up on a large stand, and sat down in a row, except for Ike, who was so amped up he had to run around the group a few times before he could sit down. Dillon Dillon, the goat, trotted in behind them, and climbed a ramp to the upper tier of the stand, directly above the dogs. Pam walked to the center of the ring with the hula hoop.

"Busker!" she cried, and the Jack Russell sprang off the stand and raced over to her. He jumped through the hoop, which was about two feet off the ground. Then he jumped back through it. Pam held out her hand in front of her. Busker sprang up, kicked off her hand, and did a back flip, landing perfectly. We all clapped and cheered. After a few more jumping tricks, she pointed him back to the stand.

"Dingo!" she shouted. She turned to face us, with her back to the dogs. She spread her feet slightly and put her hands on her hips. "Has anyone seen Dingo?" she asked, looking around. Dingo poked his head between her ankles, and then carefully placed his right paw on her right foot, and his left paw on her left foot. Pam pretended not to notice him, took a few steps forward, and then slowly turned around, making a show of looking for the dog. Dingo stayed right with her, not missing a step. "Dingo," she shouted. "Where did you go?"

Dingo stepped back and jumped through the hoop that was sticking out from her hip. He danced around in front of her, as she pretended to be surprised to see him. It was a fun skit, and one that I knew small kids would enjoy. Dingo sat down while Pam arranged two brightly colored hurdles near the center of the ring. The hurdles consisted of a top bar, which was about two feet off the ground, and then a second bar about halfway down. When she was ready, she called Dingo back over.

"Dingo, jump!" she cried. Dingo jumped over the hurdles and raced back to the stand. Busker was already on his way over, and he also jumped both hurdles.

"Ike, jump high" Pam called. Ike raced over and jumped the lower bar on each hurdle.

"Bongo!' Pam called. "Bongo, go high!" Bongo trotted over, made a beeline for the hurdles and ran right underneath them, never breaking stride. He returned to the stand. We laughed and cheered as Pam made a bow, sweeping her arm over to include the dogs.

Pam went to the gate and brought the horses in. The one with the pad trotted to the center of the ring and hopped up on the big round stool there. The other horse galloped around the perimeter of the ring. The head on the cowboy dummy bobbed back and forth, and his raised arm twitched back and forth with each stride. I couldn't decide if he was waving to the crowd or riding a rodeo bronco. Either way, it was hilarious. He made two circuits of the ring, and on the second one, Pam gave him a command. He stopped every few feet and spun in a circle. Again, the jangling piano music added zest and humor to the spectacle.

After the cowboy horse left the ring, the other one hopped down off the center stand and trotted over to the edge and began his own circuit of the perimeter.

"Zoey!" Pam called, pointing to the horse. Zoey raced across the ring, jumped up on a stool near the edge, and jumped onto the horse as the it trotted by. She landed perfectly on the big pad. They trotted around the ring, and as they approached our side, the horse trotted under a tall stand. Zoey jumped up on top of it. The horse came out the other side and continued around the ring.

"Busker!" Pam shouted. Busker raced over to the stool on the edge and sprang onto the horse. When they got around to the bridge, Busker jumped up on top. When the horse came out the other side, Zoey, who had been patiently waiting, jumped back onto the horse. When they got around to the stool at the edge, Zoey jumped down to the stool, then raced back to the stand with the other dogs. The horse continued the circle.

"Dillon Dillon," called Pam. "Let's go!" Dillon scampered down his ramp and trotted over to the stool at the edge. By this time, the horse was back to the bridge, where Busker was waiting. The horse came out from under the bridge, but Busker missed his cue. The horse trotted on without him.

"Whoa," Pam said, giving commands to the horse. It stopped and backed up to the bridge.

"Busker, down," Pam said. This time he made it, and the show resumed. We were all giggling like little kids. When they got around to where Dillon Dillon was waiting, Busker jumped to the ground, and Dillon Dillon jumped up on the horse.

"Wow," Erica said. "Now *that's* impressive."

Dillon Dillon sprang up onto the bridge, sauntered across, and hopped back onto the horse. They trotted around the ring again, and then to the center stand. The horse put his left hoof out in front of him and dropped his head down in a very impressive bow, while Dillon Dillon sat back on his haunches and raised a front hoof up in a wave. We all cheered wildly, and Pam took a bow of her own.

"That was amazing!" Amber said, holding her sides. "I laughed so much my cheeks hurt!"

"Me, too," I agreed. "I don't think I could have taken much more."

"I can't believe she trained a goat to do all that," Erica said. "I've never seen a goat that listened to anyone."

"I absolutely love his name," I said. "I can't imagine how she came up with 'Dillon Dillon' but it's the best goat name I've ever heard."

"I think Bongo is adorable," Amber said. "I want to take him home so bad I can't stand it."

Once Pam got everyone returned to their places, and got the horses unsaddled, she and Dave came over to chat for a few minutes and finish the necessary paperwork. We wished them well on their upcoming season, exchanged hugs with everyone, and headed back to the office.

"Thank you so much for bringing me along," I said to Erica on the ride back. "That was absolutely awesome."

"Yeah, I have the best job in the world," she said.

"Nope," I disagreed. "I have the best job in the world."

Life really is wonderful when you have the best job in the world, and the best wife. Somehow, I ended up with both.

6

Those Donkeys

The day finally came when Hannah, the white circus donkey, came to live at our house. Pam drove up our dirt road pulling a long, enclosed stock trailer. I was impressed with her driving skills as she maneuvered it around, backing it up and positioning herself for an easy exit.

"Hi," I called, walking over. "It looks like you've done that once before."

"Oh, this is nothing," she said. "You should see some of the places the circus puts us." She opened the back of the trailer. "Hannah Banana, come on out."

Hannah backed off the trailer and looked around. There was a stomping sound from inside the trailer, but the rear divider was closed, so I couldn't see into the rest of it.

"Who else is in there?" I asked.

"That's the baby camel," she said. "He's staying with another friend of ours this year."

I imagined all the cars she had passed on the way over here; each of them oblivious to the fact that there was a camel a few feet away from them. The thought made me smile.

"Alright, let's go introduce Hannah to Pet," I said. Hannah was busy eating grass and didn't seem particularly interested in going to meet anyone.

"She's in hog heaven right now," Pam said. "You've got much better grass here than we do." She tugged on the lead rope to get Hannah's attention, and we started off towards the back field.

Hannah and Pet hit it off immediately. They sniffed each other for a minute, muzzle to muzzle, and then slowly down the side of each other. Since Pet is a traditional brown donkey, and Hannah is white, I decided that they made a donkey yin yang, the way they were standing. Pet turned and raced across the field, and Hannah followed right behind her. Donkeys don't run like horses, which look smooth, athletic and streamlined when they run. Donkeys run with their head held straight up, nose high, ears pricked up, and tail out. It's hilarious to watch.

Millie, the retired thoroughbred that Pet had been sharing the field with for years, didn't seem at all interested in meeting Hannah. She watched everything from her vantage point at the water bucket but made no move to join in the introductions.

"Millie is being true to form," I said. "At least now she'll have an excuse to ignore Pet, and vice versa."

"They aren't real tight, huh?" Pam asked.

"Oh, they are, but from a distance," I said. "They keep a lot of space between them and pretend to ignore one another, but if you take one of them out of the field and up to the barn, the other one goes crazy and starts screaming and running the fence line. It's a hoot."

"It looks like Hannah has found her long-lost soul sister," Pam said. The donkeys had stopped running and were grazing side by side in the shade near the back of the pasture. "She's going to be fat before long."

Pet is pretty fat, which always amazes me because all she eats is grass in the summer, and hay in the winter. She is the most efficient grass-processing machine on the planet. Who else can gain so much weight eating salads? Millie, on the other hand, was a twenty-eight-year-old thoroughbred, and we had to shovel the high-end grain to her just to keep her alive. Thoroughbreds are naturally skinny, and it gets worse as they get old.

That evening, Clu got introduced to Hannah. Clu spends his days in a stall in the barn, and his nights out back with Millie and Pet. He gave Hannah a brief sniff and wandered off to graze. That's about par for Clu. Also an old-timer, he's mainly interested in eating and napping.

Everything was quiet for several weeks. Hannah and Pet were joined at the hip. The horses ignored them, and they ignored the horses. I did notice that rocks started appearing in the water bucket in their field, and I determined that was one of the ways that Hannah amused herself.

The field in-between the back pastures and the barn is the riding arena. It has fence on three sides, and the fourth side is about two thirds woods, and one third open space.

The open space is a long sweeping lawn that leads past the woods and up to the barn. When the grass in the arena gets tall, we run a temporary electric fence across the open area from the woods to the pasture fence. When Clu is out there at night, we open up their gate and let them graze in the arena as well as their pasture. This is a system that Erica has been using for years, with great success.

I will go ahead and admit that I grossly underestimated Hannah in terms of guile, intelligence, conniving nature, imagination, work ethic, and skill. All of my donkey experience had been with Pet up to that point. Pet was born right here in Alachua County, and has lived in two places over the course of her life. Pet is content to not expend a lot of energy most of the time, and she's less than ambitious. When I'm out in her field fixing a fence or trimming trees, she will usually follow me around, as she is curious, and she also loves getting her ears, neck and chest scratched, and I am a willing scratcher.

Hannah, on the other hand, is a circus donkey. I might have assumed that her disposition would be as unadventurous as Pet's, but I was wrong. I should have paid more attention to the rocks in the water bucket. Hannah has spent her life traveling all over the United States and Canada. She has forgotten more tricks than most dogs will ever learn. She knows how to work a crowd, and she knows how to get what she wants. I was soon to learn this lesson.

One morning, perhaps three or four weeks after Hannah's arrival, I went downstairs to feed, as I generally do about seven o'clock. Halfway down the stairs I stopped, turned around, and went back up to the porch and looked out. There, standing in the front yard, on the wrong side of the electric fence, stood Hannah and Pet, grazing away like everything was normal. Pet had a small tree branch stuck in her mane, which I could see from the porch.

I went downstairs, trying to figure out the best way to handle the situation. Clu and Millie were still on the other side of the fence, as they should be, but Clu needed to come into the barn, which he does unassisted each morning. I normally open the gate and let him out, and he walks into his stall and eats breakfast. I decided that Clu was going to have to come in before I could get the donkeys back on that side. I got a bucket of grain for Millie and headed out.

As I neared the donkeys, I could see that they were both covered in leaves and pine needles. They also had twigs and sticks stuck in their manes and tails. Pet looked up at me with her best innocent expression.

"Don't even try to convince me that nothing is going on," I said. "I can tell you two blazed a trail through the woods. You brought half the woods out with you."

I walked on past them to the gate portion of the electric fence. Clu was waiting on the other side, as he usually does. I opened the gate and let him through. He took a bite of Millie's grain, as is also his custom, and then headed for the barn. I shook the grain bucket, trying to entice the donkeys to follow me in with Millie.

Hannah is less food-motivated than Pet, and Pet broke almost immediately. She trotted over to me, and I rewarded her with a bite of Millie's grain.

"Come on Hannah," I coaxed. "Come get a bite of grain." She walked towards me, and I gave her a nibble. I began walking out towards the pasture gate. They followed me willingly enough and soon I had everyone where they were supposed to be.

I found the trail they had made through the woods. I shook my head, marveling at the fact that no one had ever thought to brave the thorny vines and dense undergrowth in the woods to get around the electric fence in the ten years that Erica had lived here. Hannah had a trail blazed in a few weeks.

I got some more fencing material and extended the electric fence part of the way down the wood line, blocking their entrance. The next morning, everyone was still on the proper side of the fence, and after several successful days like that, I stopped worrying about it. Again, I underestimated Hannah. It wasn't that she was being good, it was just that she had a much longer distance to get through the woods, and trail-building takes time.

About two weeks later, I went downstairs to go for a run before bringing the horses in and feeding. Erica wasn't feeling well, so I told her to stay in bed while I exercised and took care of the horses. As I stood at the bottom of the stairs stretching, some movement in the corner of my eye got my attention. I looked, and there was Pet, standing in front of the barn, all alone and looking totally guilty.

"Pet, what are you doing?" I asked, walking over to her. Again, she had twigs, leaves, and all manner of incriminating evidence covering her. Hannah was on the other side of the fence, watching smugly. "Did Hannah put you up to this? Did she talk you into coming over here, and then leave you to take the blame?" I scratched her ears, trying to decide whether to deal with it now, or after my run.

"I tell you what," I said to Pet. "You hang out here while I run down the driveway, and when I get back, we'll get you back out in your field." She didn't object, so off I went.

When I got back, there were two donkeys grazing in front of the porch. I ran upstairs and traded my running shoes for my rubber boots, then came back down. I grabbed a bucket of grain for Millie, hoping to recreate my successful model from the last time. I shook the bucket to let them know I had food, and headed out towards the gate where Clu stood waiting.

As Clu started out the gate, I heard a thundering of hooves, and I was surprised to see Millie come flying past us. She sailed right on by the barn. Clu bucked and farted a few times, then took off after her. Not to be outdone, the donkeys took off right behind them, heads held high. I stood there holding the gate in one hand, and the feed bucket in the other. Somehow, in the space of five seconds, I was the only one there.

I left the gate open and headed around the barn. I could tell from the sound of half a dozen whinnying horses that they were out at the front pastures getting everyone riled up. As soon as I got in sight of them, I knew I was in trouble. Angie and Sydney were racing up and down the fence line in their pasture, rearing and bucking. Ernie and Gigi were doing the same thing on the other side of the driveway. I charged over to them, making shooing gestures and yelling, trying to drive the back-field crew back to their end of the farm. Clu took off around the left side of the barn. Millie went straight into the barn, galloping right down the concrete aisle. I cringed, knowing that Erica was lying in bed and would be able to hear the racket. The donkeys took off to the right and disappeared behind the mother-in-law suite. I followed the donkeys.

It's important to remember that I had just finished

running two miles, and was already hot, sweaty, and tired. It's also important to remember that I had made the questionable decision to change into my rubber boots, which I usually wear to feed so my shoes don't get soaked walking around in the dew-wet grass. Running in rubber boots is a challenge even if you aren't already tired.

When I got around the back of Elise's place, the donkeys took things to the next level. Pet spun around and ran away from me, and Hannah ran towards me, passing wide to my right and going back down to the front pastures. Pet trotted over to the front of the barn, and then took off through the barn aisle to reconnect with Hannah. Millie was over by the woods, grazing, and Clu was back out in the back pasture. I was getting nowhere.

I went to the barn and got a lunge whip. This is a whip that has a stiff plastic centerpiece for the first six feet, and then has six feet of free whip. It's a handy tool for a situation like this, as you can hold it out sideways to make yourself much wider and keep them from running by. Plus, you can also swing it. The whistle it makes going through the air is enough to get most critters motivated, and if you pop it, it will definitely get their attention. It's all threats, no contact.

I went back up front and herded the donkeys towards the barn. This involved a lot of running on my part, left and right, trying to keep them going in the desired direction. Millie wandered back into the barn aisle just as we were coming through it, and I managed to get the three of them headed out back. At the last second, Millie decided to peel off and go back up front. I leaped to that side, swinging the whip around to deter her. I don't know if it was the whistle of the whip that turned her around, or the sound of it hitting my bare, sweaty back that did it, or my screams of pain and surprise. Yes, somehow I managed to whip the shit out of myself, and it hurt. That really pissed me off and I pursued them with renewed vigor. My new level of verbal encouragement kept them moving forward, and I was grateful for that, because I was terrified of swinging the whip again. My back felt like it was on fire, and I was pretty sure it was bleeding profusely. I couldn't tell for sure if it was blood or sweat running down my back.

Once they were all through the back gate, I shut and locked it, exhausted. I was now twenty minutes behind schedule, totally out of energy, in pain, and not a single horse was in the barn. I decided to go get a halter and walk Clu in, just in case he wasn't finished acting up. I walked the rest of the upfront crew in one at a time, instead of the usual two at a time. I wasn't taking any chances now, not at this stage of things. At last they were all in their stalls, eating breakfast. I staggered up the stairs just as poor Erica came outside to see what was going on.

"So…" she began.

"Yeah, it was a disaster," I said, cutting her off. "Is my back bleeding?"

She checked me out. "Well, you've got a bright red stripe, but no blood," she said. "What happened?"

"Let's go eat breakfast. I'll tell you all about it."

7

Rescuing Highway, the I-75 Miracle Horse

It's not unusual for Erica's phone to ring first thing in the morning, but when it rings twice, back to back, that's usually a bad sign. Erica was already headed downstairs to feed the horses, and I was about to follow her down when her phone rang. I debated about letting it go, since we would be back up in about fifteen minutes, but something told me I should go grab it for her. By the time I got my boots off and made it back to the bedroom where it was charging, it had stopped ringing, but it started again as soon as I picked it up.

Deputy Henderson was the name on the screen. I knew him, as he is one of our rural services sheriff's deputies, and we work with them on a regular basis. I stepped out onto the porch and called down to Erica.

"Hey, come grab your phone. The sheriff is calling."

She stepped out from under the porch, and I dropped the phone down to her. I could only hear her side of the conversation, which was very short, but I knew immediately that we were going to an emergency. I went back inside to get dressed for work.

A moment later the front door opened, and Erica ran in. "We need to get the trailer hooked up. I'll follow you in the vet truck."

That was unusual. We rarely transport horses, so I knew this was an exceptional situation. "What's going on?"

She grabbed a scrub top out of the drawer and pulled it over her head. "They've got a horse on the side of the interstate. It looks like it's been hit by a car, but they don't know."

"Oh, no! Can it walk?"

"Well, it's standing, but that's about all I know. He said it's scraped up pretty bad."

We raced downstairs and got the truck and trailer hooked up. It was about a thirty-minute drive to where they were located, near Paynes Prairie. Our morning routine was out the window, which meant that not only were our horses missing breakfast, but we were, too. I scarfed a protein bar as I drove, going through all the possibilities that I could come up with on what might have happened. Paynes Prairie has wild horses, so one of them might have gotten past the fence somehow. There are also a lot of horse farms along the I-75 corridor, so it could have been from any one of a hundred different places if it wasn't wild.

It was also possible that the injuries they were reporting were from running through a fence, rather than getting hit by a car. Sometimes a horse will spook at something and run right through a fence, which can tear them to shreds. We've sewn up several of those, and they really do look like they've been hit by a bus when their chest and legs are hanging open in bloody flaps of skin.

We didn't have an exact location, as it was between two mile-marker posts, but there was no question about where they were when we got close. There were so many strobe lights flashing on the other side of the median that you couldn't help but look. I had to go about a quarter of a mile past them to get to a cut through in the median to get turned around. Fortunately, it was still early, about 7:45 am, so traffic wasn't too bad. I pulled past the state trooper and the three county deputies, and parked just off the shoulder, leaving room behind me for Erica to park the vet truck.

The horse was standing down in the ditch as we walked up, and the rural services deputy had a halter on him. He was scratching the horse's head and talking softly to him, trying to keep him calm as the traffic thundered by a few feet away.

"Hey, Doc, we got a good one for you," Deputy Henderson said with a grin. "He looks rough, but he's as calm and quiet as you could ask for."

The horse was black, with a white star on his forehead. His knees were raw and bloody, and I could see in the light from Erica's headlamp that the wound on the right knee was deep and filled with bits of gravel and asphalt. He certainly didn't get that from running through a fence.

His flank had a bloody scrape, and when she pushed his rear end over a step to get the sunlight on it, there was no doubt that he had slid down the road. His coat was scraped away on all the protruding points where his abdomen was in contact with the ground, with blood seeping through the abrasions. There was also a big abrasion high above his shoulder where the bone of his shoulder had nearly worn through the skin as he slid. He had a variety of other cuts and scrapes, one of them a pretty deep gash on his shoulder, as well some abrasions on his face.

The other cops stood in a group nearby, watching silently as Erica checked out the horse. It was weird to see them all deferring to Erica, as the cops are usually the ones in charge of a situation, but it was quickly clear that they were waiting for her to make decisions and form a plan.

I stepped over beside the state trooper. "How's the car that hit him?" I asked. "Did anyone get hurt?"

"We've got nothing," he said. "No wrecked vehicle, no reports of anyone hitting anything, just a couple of calls about a horse standing on the side of the road."

"Really?" I was surprised. A black horse on a black road in the dark would be easy to hit, but I couldn't imagine anyone driving away from that. "That's interesting."

The trooper shrugged. "Any number of reasons why somebody might not want to call it in. DUI, suspended license, outstanding warrant, drugs in the car, lapsed insurance, you name it. Even fear of getting sued can keep people from reporting something."

That made me rethink things. My universe gets pretty small, and sometimes I forget that other people aren't having the same experience in life that I am. "I guess I can see that."

Erica was wrapping up her physical exam, so I stepped back over in case she needed me to grab something.

"Have you moved him at all?" Erica asked.

The deputy shook his head. "He was standing here when I spotted him. He let me walk right up and put a halter on him."

"Okay. Most of this is superficial, but I'm worried about his knees. Let's see if he can take a few steps."

Deputy Henderson led him forward a few steps, and he willingly followed, though slowly and with a limp. "He seems to be putting weight on it okay."

"Yeah, I think so," Erica said. "Do we have an owner yet?"

Henderson shook his head. "Nope, and no microchip. He definitely didn't come from Paynes Prairie, though, he's too tame. Somebody ought to be missing him when they feed this morning, so we'll probably get a call about it soon."

"Alright. Let me give him some pain medication so he's not hurting so bad, and then we'll get him on the trailer and back to the clinic. Once we have an owner, we can make some treatment decisions."

"You think that knee is going to be okay, Doc?" Henderson asked.

Erica shook her head. "Not likely, unless they're willing to spend a lot of money. That joint is wide open, and it'll take surgery to get all the asphalt out of there, maybe more than one. Even then, it's a coin toss. I guarantee it'll get infected."

That was bad. Leg joints are the Achilles Heel for horses, and if they get infected, it can easily kill them. This guy was in a race against time, assuming someone was willing to pay for him to have surgery to flush his joints, and spend months rehabbing him.

I jogged back to the vet truck with Erica. "What do you think?"

She grabbed a syringe and drew some medicine out of a small, clear bottle. "This is probably going to end up as a euthanasia, but we'll at least get him off the highway and make him feel better."

"That's a tough way to go." I shook my head. "Surviving getting hit by a car, then dying of infection."

"I don't think he got hit by a vehicle," she said. "He's hurt, but not in the right way for that. He slid down the road for sure, but there isn't any impact trauma."

"What does that leave?" I asked. "Could he get all that from running down the road and falling?"

"Maybe," she said. "Or he could have come off a trailer, if it wasn't going very fast." We hurried back to the horse, and Erica gave him a shot.

"Okay, we're ready to load him," she said. "I don't know how hard that's going to be, with all these cars going by."

"We'll block traffic," Deputy Henderson said. "You get the trailer as close as you can, and we'll shut down the right two lanes, just to be on the safe side."

The other cops split off to their cars and began arranging themselves down the road, funneling traffic over to the far lane. I hopped in the truck and backed along the shoulder until I was almost even with the horse. Once again, the trailer-backing skills I'd acquired so many years ago were coming into play as I maneuvered around the vet truck and pointed the trailer slightly downhill towards the horse. I felt an odd thrill as I opened the trailer door. The people creeping by were staring at us, and even though I was just the ambulance driver, it was very exciting to be involved.

Deputy Henderson carefully led the horse up the embankment. Erica and I walked behind him, and the

remaining deputy stood on the shoulder of the interstate.

"Go easy," Erica said, as they reached the back of the trailer. "He might not be able to get up there, and I don't want to make him panic and try to bolt."

"Got it," Henderson said. He stepped inside the trailer and turned around to face the horse, clucking softly. "Come on, boy. What do you think?"

The horse nickered and stepped right up into the trailer bedside him. Erica and I shared a surprised glance.

"Wow," I said, swinging the door closed as Henderson stepped out. "That was easier than I expected."

We all grinned at one another, relieved that nothing terrible happened.

"Good job, everybody," Erica said. "Justin, head on back to the clinic. Remember, super-easy on the starts and stops, and the turns. I'm going to head home and feed our crew. Dr. Allison will handle this guy. I'll call her and fill her in on the way back, and they'll be ready when you get there."

I pulled onto the highway, accelerating slowly. Traffic was still in the third lane over, so I didn't have to worry about getting rear-ended as we slowly got up to speed. A moment later, Deputy Henderson caught up to me and stayed back there. There were sure to be some frustrated people behind us once we got into town and left the interstate, as it was now the height of morning rush hour, but they would just have to deal with it. The drive to the clinic was slow, but thankfully uneventful.

When we arrived, the clinic staff was ready and waiting for us. I backed right up to the aisleway, and by the time I got out of the truck, they had the trailer door open and were easing the horse back out and onto the floor. Dr. Allison

and the techs went right to work cleaning his wounds, and Deputy Henderson and I stood by, watching and waiting.

By the time they had him cleaned up and the scrapes treated, it was nearly 10:00 am. Despite the extent of his injuries, the horse was bright-eyed and receptive to the attention the techs were giving him. Dr. Allison walked over to us, peeling off her gloves.

"Still no word on the owner?" she asked.

The deputy shook his head. "Nope, this is pretty crazy, but we haven't heard a peep."

"Well, we're at the point where we have to make some decisions." Dr. Allison put her hands on her hips. "I've done what I can to make him comfortable and treat the small stuff."

I spoke up. "What do you all think about putting this on Facebook? We can post a video of him on the clinic page and explain the situation. Somebody might recognize him."

Deputy Henderson pulled his phone out. "I gotta call in on that one. I don't know what the rules are in a situation like this."

He stepped away, and I turned back to Dr. Allison. "The next step is surgery, right?"

She shook her head. "No, I could do a joint perfusion, and run some antibiotics in there. That would buy us a little time. He'll still need surgery to get all the asphalt out, but we can start on the infection side of things now. It's either that, or we need to euthanize him."

Since he was technically in the custody of the sheriff's department, it would be their call, but they couldn't accept financial responsibility for a surgery. Whatever we did would be at our own financial risk.

"What are we looking at on a perfusion, pricewise, if the owner doesn't want to pay?" I asked, as the deputy walked back over.

"Probably a couple hundred dollars," she said. "What do you want to do?"

Deputy Henderson spoke up. "We got permission to put it on Facebook to try and find the owner, but we can't pay for anything. There's no budget for something like this."

"Go ahead and do the perfusion," I said. "We need more time. If the owner doesn't want to pay for it, we'll deal with it, but it's not fair to the horse to put off antibiotics when we know he's going to die of infection if we wait too long. I don't think we have any other choice."

"We could euthanize," Dr. Allison said. "The way his knee joint is damaged, it's certainly an option. I wouldn't give him great odds of surviving this, even if we went to surgery right now."

We looked at one another, then looked at the horse, the silence hanging in the air between us like a heavy curtain. He was eating treats from one of the techs, nuzzling her palm and nickering softly as she scratched his ears. No one wanted to give him a death sentence.

"Not yet," I said. "Let's do the antibiotics and get this on Facebook. If we don't have an owner by noon, we'll make a decision."

They nodded, and the team got to work again. While they were working on the horse, I took a few pictures of him and got to work with the office crew on a Facebook post.

"We need a name," Amy said. "What are we going to call him?"

"He's like a teddy bear," Rachel said. "He's super cuddly."

"There you go," Dr. Allison chimed in. "Teddy Bear Highway."

We decided to do a Facebook Live video explaining what happened to Teddy Bear Highway and asking if anyone knew who he belonged to. That would reach the most people in the shortest amount of time. As soon as it was up, the sheriff's department shared the video on their page, and the post went viral almost immediately.

They finished the joint perfusion a bit later, and Dr. Allison removed a few more bits of asphalt and gravel from the joint as they washed out from deeper inside. It was amazing to see the pile of stuff that came out of his knee. The antibiotics were administered in a bag of IV fluids above the knee, and as it came down into the joint, it carried debris that couldn't be seen from the surface.

Noon was fast approaching, and we still didn't have an owner located. Our Facebook video had been seen and shared by thousands of people. The sheriff's department had used every resource available to them, but neither one of us had come up with anything. We had to do something; Highway was running out of time.

By this point, everyone at the clinic had developed an attachment to him. He was unbelievably kind and easy-going, despite the incredibly tough day he'd had. Erica returned from another appointment, and we all gathered in front of his stall with Deputy Henderson.

"Well, we're in a tough spot," Henderson said. "The county can't cover his medical expenses. If this is it, then we've got no choice but to euthanize him."

My heart felt like a stone had been dropped on it. There had to be another way out of this. Highway whinnied softly on the other side of the stall door, and we all turned to look at him as one.

"Maybe the clinic can adopt him," Lily said. "We've got cats, why not a horse?"

I didn't want to be the one to explain that we didn't have the money to send him to a referral hospital for surgery. That would cost at least six thousand dollars, and maybe a lot more.

"We could raise money with a Go Fund Me campaign," Amy said. "That way the county wouldn't have to force the euthanasia."

We looked at one another, and then turned to the deputy. "Is that an option?" Erica asked.

He held up a finger and pulled out his phone. "I'm not making that decision. Hang on a minute."

He turned away and had a brief conversation with someone. A moment later he was back, a grin reaching across his face. "They said go for it. The Facebook post has had too much interaction to euthanize him now. He's turning into a celebrity."

We all cheered, and Amy hurried inside to get it set up.

"How do we do this?" I asked Erica. "Should I get going with him now? It's going to take us forty-five minutes to get to the hospital."

"Let's wait a minute," she said. "This might not work. I don't want to get him on the surgery table down there and find out we only raised a hundred dollars. That wouldn't be fair to anyone."

My shoulders sagged, but I knew she was right. Just because tons of people had shared our post didn't guarantee they would be willing to chip in for his surgery. Amy poked her head around the corner and called to us down the hallway.

"You might want to come look at this."

We hurried down to her office. She had two windows open on her computer screen. One was the Go Fund Me page, and the other was Facebook.

"It's only been up for twenty minutes," Amy said. "We've already raised over a thousand dollars. We've also had three calls from clients pledging money for him. Look at the Facebook post. It's going crazy!"

"Wow!" Erica and I looked at one another, and she shrugged. "Okay, so let me call EMC and get this set up with them. It looks like you're going."

By the time we got Highway loaded in the trailer, we had over two thousand dollars raised. When I got him to EMC less than an hour later, it was at three thousand dollars.

We decided that we had to keep everyone informed of what was happening, since so many people had stepped forward to save his life. I did another Facebook Live video as he came off the trailer and went into the surgery unit at EMC. It was a little bit scary, putting everything we did out for the public eye to scrutinize, but it was the only way we could keep Highway alive.

Highway made it through his first surgery with flying colors and stayed at EMC for a few days to recover. We stopped the Go Fund Me when it hit $9,000. We were stunned that so many people had donated to it. It wasn't just local people who had seen it on Facebook or on the news, we had people from all over the world donating. I couldn't believe it.

While all that was happening, the sheriff's department had been working hard to figure out who he belonged to. The Facebook campaign had been seen by people all over the country, and someone commented on one of the posts that Highway had belonged to them years before. Soon after that, another former owner popped up, and then another.

By the time I went down to EMC a few days later to bring Highway back to our clinic to recover, Deputy Henderson had a pretty clear picture of what had happened. It wasn't a happy story, but it made it exceedingly clear that Highway was one lucky guy.

It's always risky selling a horse, because you never know what's going to happen to them down the road. Lots of horses end up in bad situations due to a variety of reasons. Sometimes their owners fall on hard times and can't afford to take care of them anymore. Sometimes owners pass away, and the horses end up being sold to whoever will take them. Sometimes there's just an unfortunate series of events that take place.

Butchering horses is illegal in the United States, but in many other countries it's common, no different than butchering cows or pigs. Because of this, there are people who make a living going to auctions and buying unwanted horses. They then take these horses to Mexico and sell them for meat.

Highway had been sold several times over the years. The last time was a few months before this took place, and the woman who bought him had a lot of trouble with him. He was wonderful in every way until she tried to ride him in an arena, at which time he would buck, run away, whatever he could do to stop her from being on him. Some of his previous owners confirmed that they had the same problem with him. I don't know what his reason was, but he didn't want to be a competitor anymore.

His current owner told the sheriff that she didn't want someone to get hurt trying to ride Highway, so she found a guy who told her he would euthanize the horse for free. We'll call him Wilbur. She dropped Highway off at Wilbur's house and returned home under the impression that it was over. Instead of killing Highway, Wilbur loaded him on a trailer with several other horses the next day and took off for an auction to sell them.

It was early in the morning when he left, still dark. We don't exactly what happened, but for some reason Wilbur stopped on the side of the highway. When he took off again, the trailer door came open, and Highway, who was on the back of the trailer, either jumped or fell out as the truck accelerated away. They couldn't have been going very fast, probably not more than 25 mph based on Highway's injuries, but apparently Wilbur didn't realize what was happening, and he continued to drive.

Highway fell when he hit the asphalt, sliding down the road on his knees, then rolling over on one side and all the way onto his back before coming to a stop. The pain must have been tremendous, both from slamming into the highway at that speed, and from the road rash that immediately followed. He scrambled to his feet, probably falling again a few times on the slippery asphalt, and somehow made his way off the side of the road before the next car came by. He stood there in the darkness, alone and suffering, but alive.

A truck driver caught up with Wilbur in the truck at some point. The trailer door was still wide open as he drove down the interstate, other horses visible inside. The truck driver honked his horn and flashed his lights, finally getting Wilbur to pull over. Wilbur later told the sheriff that he looked around, but couldn't find Highway anywhere, so he closed the trailer door, got back in his truck and drove on to the auction. A witness claimed to have seen him pull over, close the trailer, and drive away.

As daylight began to creep into the sky, several passing motorists saw Highway standing beside the interstate, bloody and battered, and called 911. Shortly after that, our phone rang, and you know what happened from there. The sheriff's department did press charges against Wilbur for abandoning the horse on the Interstate and not reporting it.

Highway became internationally famous, with people all over the world following his story as it unfolded. When it came out that he was supposed to be either euthanized or sold for slaughter, we all realized that the traumatic experience of falling off a moving trailer on the interstate actually saved his life. He beat certain death by avoiding the auction, then he beat death by surviving the fall and not getting run over in the dark, then he beat death by surviving the infection in his knee. Highway was meant to live!

He stayed at our house for quite a while after his first surgery. He couldn't go out in the pastures with the other horses because his knees wouldn't be able to handle him trying to run, so he was on stall rest, which he was not happy about. I took him out to graze on a lead rope several times a day, which made him happier, and he had a steady supply of carrots coming into the vet clinic from well-wishers. He's all about a carrot.

His wounds had to be treated a lot, so he had visitors every day. It was nearing Christmas, so they decorated his bandages in the holiday spirit. His Facebook following demanded regular updates too, so he got to be featured on Facebook very frequently. He's quite the ham, so he didn't mind the attention.

Eventually the doctors decided he was stable enough to go to the Dreamcatcher Horse Ranch Rescue Center, which would become his permanent home. Shortly after getting there, the infection in his knee flared back up, and he had to have another surgery. Kate Santich of the *Orlando Sentinel* interviewed Loren Wheatley, who runs the rescue center. This excerpt is from her January 15, 2019 article:

> "They told me to say goodbye because he had a 5 percent chance, and he probably wasn't going to make it," she says, barely getting the words out. "Sorry—this part always gets hard. They said he has, um… God, this freakin' horse, man… I don't cry—ever. But… he's just… he's special."[1]

Once again, Highway beat the odds. That's four times, if you're keeping count. Highway is a survivor.

Nowadays, Highway is mostly healed. He still has physical therapy and regular veterinary appointments, where they work on his mobility and scar tissue, but he's out of the woods on the infection front. He has a best friend, loving caretakers, and a forever home. He didn't have any of that on the day he fell out of the trailer.

Highway has his own Facebook page these days, https://www.facebook.com/HighwaytheMiracleHorse/, and

---

[1] Santich, Kate. "Horse that escaped 'death sentence' now healing at Lake ranch." The Orlando Sentinel 15 Jan 2019 OrlandoSentinel.com 15 Jan 2019

he has quite a following online. Along with the other horses at the rescue center, he lives on donations, and his continued medical needs cost money. It also costs a lot just to feed a horse, keep their feet trimmed by the farrier every 5-6 weeks, and pay the electric bill for a barn. You can donate through Facebook at the link above, or go to their website: http://www.dreamcatcherhorses.com/.

Anyone who has ever worked for a rescue will tell you that it's easy to get people to donate once, but it's hard to get people to donate over and over. However, the bills roll in every month, just like yours and mine. If you'd like to help Highway, or any other 501(c)3 rescue operation, they would definitely appreciate it. $10 a month, every month, would do them far more good than $100 once, and most of us can manage that. I'm just saying.

8

Foster Parents

L iving with a veterinarian comes with certain hazards, one of which being that they are prone to coming home with animals without warning. At our house, this sometimes happens in the form of wounded horses that need some sort of medicine every hour or two. Other times it happens in the form of homeless kittens.

One particular Friday evening, we were down in the barn messing around. Erica had just gotten home, and Bridget was feeding the horses. Erica's phone rang; it was Lilly, the office assistant at the clinic. Lilly is nineteen, smart, captain of the equestrian team at the University of Florida where she is also a full-time student, and is generally exceptionally competent and amazing in everything she does.

In this situation, she did not display any of those qualities, other than being nineteen. I could hear both sides of the conversation, as there was a lot of hysterical shrieking coming from Lilly.

"Oh my God," she said, "there're baby kittens in the back of my truck! I started to pull out of the clinic, and I stopped to lock the gate, and I heard this like, weird noise in the back of my truck, and I looked in and there were these tiny baby kittens, and they're crying."

"Take a breath," Erica said.

"I don't know what to do!" She sounded like she was about to laugh hysterically, or cry, I couldn't tell which. "I'm nineteen years old; I don't know anything about babies! I'm in college, for God's sake!"

"Alright, put them in the front seat with you, and bring them over," said Erica. "We'll figure it out."

How could I have known that phone call would alter the next few weeks of my life so drastically? Lilly pulled into the yard about ten minutes later and hopped out of her truck with a five-gallon bucket, which she presented to Erica.

"There're two of them," she said, clearly relieved to turn over the responsibility to someone else.

Erica sat the bucket down, reached in, and pulled out two tiny kittens. One was calico, and one was black.

"They're barely opening their eyes," she said. "They're probably only about two weeks old."

"I don't know how they ended up in the back of my truck," said Lilly. "I mean, the clinic is outside of town on a dirt road, and you have to sit and wait for the gate to open, so I don't see how someone could have dumped them there."

"No, me either," Erica agreed. "It almost had to be the momma cat stashing them there."

"Well, there're kids that live on that road," I pointed out. "Maybe their parents sent them down to dump the kittens on our porch, since it's a vet clinic, and they chickened out and stuck them in the truck." It was a bit of a stretch, but I stood by its plausibility.

Erica's mom happened to be home that weekend, and came over to see what the fuss was all about.

"Oh, my," she said. "New additions to the family?"

I cringed at the thought. Not only do we have five cats already, but they are extremely hostile to outsiders. When Tony the Office Cat had to come home with us on the weekends due to a medication he had to have every few hours, half the cats hid in the woods all weekend on a hunger strike, and the other half tried to attack him constantly.

It's not just other cats that they are hostile to, either. When Norma Jean went to heaven, Elise found a Shih Tzu named Mimi that needed a home. Everyone fell in love with her right away except the cats. Again, half of them stayed in the woods most of the time, they all gave her a very wide berth and a lot of hissing whenever they came near one another (which was often, in a seven hundred square foot apartment), and she got swatted with claws out whenever she tried to make friends with them for the first three months she was here.

I considered all of that in the two-second pause that everyone took after Elise's question, and I realized they were all trying to gauge my reaction.

"Well, we have a pretty big Facebook network, so I'm sure we'll find them a good forever home in the next few days." I felt like it was a safe, diplomatic approach to the situation. Erica was still checking them over.

"Mom, can you go get some milk replacer?" she asked. "I think we still have some bottles somewhere, right?"

"We've got two bottles in the cabinet where the glasses are," Elise said. "Do you want me to get anything else while I'm out?"

"Nope, I think we have everything else, for now." Erica glanced at me. "We can start looking for homes for them, but they can't go until they're off the bottles and on to solid food, and that's going to be a few weeks."

"Okay, no worries," I said. "I don't mind bottle-feeding a baby kitten. In fact, it'll probably be fun!"

"They have to eat every two hours," she said. I felt like I detected a faint, smug satisfaction in her voice, but it was hard to tell with the way my spirits were plunging.

"Every two hours? Like, twelve times a day, around the clock?"

"Yep," she confirmed with a grin. "And you're right, it will be fun!"

I felt like something terrible had just happened.

"Oh my God," said Lilly. "I'm so glad you know what to do with them. I wouldn't have known to do all that."

"Are you sure you don't want to take them home?" I asked her with a chuckle. "This would be a great way to find out if you want to have kids in the future."

"No thanks, I can already tell it's more than I want to get into," she said with a laugh. "I can't even keep up with homework and riding club and keeping Eeyore the Trouble Donkey from destroying the neighborhood."

"So, the calico is a girl, of course, and the black one is a boy," Erica announced. She handed the boy to me.

He pretty much fit in my hand. His fur was super soft, and so black that it seemed to have a bluish tint in the sunlight. His ears were disproportionately huge, dwarfing his head, and his eyes seemed conversely small.

"Hey, little buddy," I said, running a finger down his back. "I'm going to call you Radar. What do you think about that?"

"Mew, mew, mew" he replied. It seemed to be a positive response.

"Well, this one seems like a Zoey," Erica said. "Zoey and Radar, calico and black."

I handed Radar back to Erica. "We're going to have to figure out a nest for them," I said. "I'll go pack up the music gear in the spare bedroom and make some space."

I used to be in a band, in which I wrote songs, sang, and played guitar. I also acted as our recording engineer, and recorded a lot of our original music. I still have all the stuff, and sometimes I get nostalgic and set up the PA system in the spare bedroom and mess around. I had recently had one of those urges, so there were speakers, amplifiers, microphones, and that kind of stuff all over the room at the moment. After packing up the guitars, the keyboard, and rolling up cables, I stashed everything in the closet, and carried the speakers downstairs to the tack room. I hadn't intended to put it all away, but I didn't know how quickly the kittens would start climbing everything, and I didn't want anything getting damaged.

I found a large cardboard box in the garage, and I made a pallet of towels in it. I put a small, shallow cardboard box filled with kitty litter in one corner, and a shallow water dish. Elise returned with the milk replacer just as I was finishing up.

Erica heated some water in the microwave, added the powdered milk, and brought the two bottles back to the spare bedroom. Elise followed with the kittens. I had a stack of extra towels on the spare bed, and I put one on the floor beside me, just in case. I've been pooped on before, and it doesn't hurt to be cautious.

As it turns out, I was worried about all the wrong things. Erica handed Radar to me and sat down in front of me with Zoey. I held Radar with one hand and tried to steer the nipple into his mouth with the other hand. It sounds simple enough, right? Wrong.

Radar was really hungry, but he had no idea what a bottle was. He twisted and squirmed, and turned his head away. In the process of evading the nipple, he managed to free some milk from the bottle, which he got all over his face. I guess the smell registered as food, because he licked his face, and got a taste of it. I took advantage of his mouth being open and tried to jam the nipple in it. A bit more milk squirted out, but the nipple turned to the side and slipped out the corner of his mouth.

At this point, he knew there was milk in the bottle, and he wanted it. With all four paws, he latched on to my hand, sinking his claws into my skin as he jammed his head at the side of the nipple, and the side of the bottle, and everywhere except the business end of the nipple. My hand was on fire, and because he was latched onto the hand that was holding the bottle, I couldn't steer it to try and help him out. There is no intensity like that of a starving kitten, and I was amazed out how ferocious he was in his attempts to get the milk.

Erica wasn't having any better luck. Zoey was mewing and struggling, and was shredding Erica's hand the same way that Radar was destroying mine. That made me feel a little better about my feeding failure. I attempted to disengage my hand from the claws, which was almost impossible, as there were four paws, and I only had one hand to use. As soon as I got one paw loose and let go of it, he latched right back on.

I changed tactics, drawing my knees up to my chest. I slowly transitioned him from my hand to my knee, and with a bit of adjusting, I managed to get him clinging to my leg to hold himself up, which kept his paws busy, and put his head on top of my knee, which positioned him just right. I supported his body and held his head still against my leg with one hand, and guided the bottle in with the other hand. Success! In seconds, he was happily gurgling milk like he'd been doing it forever. That time. It turned out that he had a short memory, but I wouldn't find that out for another two hours.

I'm a morning person. My eyes usually pop open between four-thirty and five every morning, and that's when I get up, pour a cup of coffee, and get my day going. Because of this morning schedule, I'm usually in bed by nine-thirty most nights, unable to keep my eyes open. Erica, on the other hand, is a night person. She was fine at the ten pm feeding, and I was tired. I had to struggle with Radar to get the nipple in his mouth, but I felt better about the positioning technique I had worked out earlier.

At the midnight feeding, I was not enthusiastic about having the kittens anymore.

At the two a.m. feeding, I was completely over the kittens.

"I want to retract Radar's name and give him a number to show that I am over him," I said. "I was thinking about calling him Eight."

"Eight?" Erica asked.

"Eight," I confirmed. "Twelve feedings a day minus the four hours of sleep he has cost me tonight."

"That's ridiculous," she replied.

"I'm not surprised," I said. "I can't think very clearly because I'm sleeping an hour and a half at a time. I'll come up with a better one tomorrow."

At the four a.m. feeding, I was torn as to whether I should go back to bed, or just make the coffee and stay up. I felt like a zombie. I was exhausted, my hand had about a hundred puncture wounds, and I couldn't think straight. I went back to bed.

The six a.m. feeding went better. I had coffee with that one, and coffee can make a lot of bad things better. I apologized to Radar about the whole name retraction thing.

"Look man, you've got to appreciate my position," I reasoned with him. "I have to get up for a horse emergency now and then, but that's usually all at one shot, not getting up over and over all night. Erica does that, but I've escaped it so far. This is all new to me, and I need a chance to get in the groove."

"Mew," said Radar. I felt like he got it.

The next night went largely the same. I was glad it was the weekend, because I was totally lethargic.

"Alright, I want to make a deal," I told Erica. We were sitting on the floor of the spare bedroom feeding kittens, which is all I could remember doing forever.

"What deal is that?" she asked.

"In an effort to let us both get some sleep tonight so we can function at work tomorrow, let's take turns feeding. You feed at ten, since you'll still be awake anyway. I'll do it at midnight, you at two, and me at four. That way we each only have to get up once."

"Can you feed them both at the same time?" she asked.

"I've got two knees, and there are two kittens. We'll make it work."

"Alright, you got a deal," she said. We did a fist bump, making it official.

After that it got a lot better, at least in terms of feeding. The new challenge became finding them. By the end of the first week, they were cruising everywhere. They hid under the bed, they climbed the side of the bed, they climbed on top of the books on the bookshelves, they climbed everywhere. I was relieved that I had put all my music gear away before this development took place.

We began to let them out into the rest of the house during the evenings, much to the horror of the rest of the cats. The dogs didn't care, but there was a full-on cat revolt. I was amazed to see Pesca and Ari so terrified of the tiny, helpless kittens.

"You two were that size just a few years ago," Erica told them. "Now you know how Ofeibea felt."

They did not appear to empathize with Ofeibea, nor did they relax about the kittens.

"Don't get so worked up," I told them. "We'll either find a home for them, or a home for you. Either way, it's a temporary problem."

"Hey, don't listen to him," Erica jumped in. "You two aren't going anywhere."

I tried to give them a stern eye, but they were too busy hissing at the kittens to notice.

As the kittens got bigger, they got more ferocious and

aggressive with the bottles at feeding time. I started wearing leather gloves when I fed them to protect my hands. I was in much worse shape than Erica, as I was doing all of the day feedings, and she only had to deal with the claws two or three times a day.

Things got interesting again when we started introducing canned food to them. Radar loved it, but Zoey was slow to accept the idea that it was food. We mixed milk in with it to help her out. Once she was eating it without being coerced into it, we were able to cut back on the number of feedings and increase the sleep. That was a relief!

One day I lost Radar. I was sitting at my desk working, and the kittens were running around the living room, as had become the routine. I glanced over to check on them, and I only saw Zoey. That was not too surprising, as one of them was usually crawling around under the couch, or behind the chair, or under the desk. I needed a break anyway, so I got up and got a drink of water.

"Radar, where are you hiding?" I called. No response.

I looked in the usual places, but there was no Radar. I looked back in the bedrooms: no Radar. I glanced in the bathroom, and checked the laundry room: again, no Radar. I began to get concerned.

I searched the living room thoroughly this time, using the flashlight feature on my phone to see clearly behind and under the couch and chair. Radar was nowhere to be found. I tried to remember that last time I had actually seen him. Was it before lunch? I had gone out on the front porch at lunch time. Had he slipped out the door without me noticing? I was suddenly sure that he had wandered out and fell off the porch, having no concept of depth and distance.

I raced outside and hastily searched the porch before running downstairs. I was working myself up towards a panic, imagining the injuries he might have from a ten-foot fall. I searched all around the shrubs, not finding him anywhere. It was possible that he might have landed in some of the plants and been unharmed, at which point he could have wandered off anywhere. My eye was instantly drawn to the woods at that thought. I did a quick search of the barn, trying to keep myself in a rational frame of mind. I looked in each of the stalls, bracing myself for the sight of a little black fur ball sticking out from under a hoof, but I didn't find him in a stall. That was a relief. I did a circuit of the exterior of the barn with no luck.

At last, I decided I was going to have to search the woods. That is no small task, as I've had to go find a full-grown cat in there many times, and it's difficult to spot them. Seeing a small black cat in the woods would be even more difficult. I knew better than to go into the woods in a pair of shorts. The thorn-covered vines would tear my legs to shreds, and I would probably end up with poison ivy. I ran back up the stairs to put on a pair of pants.

I opened the door and walked into the kitchen. Zoey and Radar were playing in the middle of the floor, wrestling with each other over one of the cat toys. I scooped them up to put them in the bedroom for safe keeping while I was in the woods looking for Radar, when I realized that I was holding Radar.

"Radar! Where in the hell have you been hiding?" I exclaimed, stopping in my tracks. "I've been worried sick about you!"

"Mew," he replied, climbing my shirt. He had taken a

liking to my beard, and he often climbed up to rub his face on it lately, as he was doing now. I think it was a diversion tactic, and a fairly effective one, as I stopped being annoyed with him almost immediately.

"I know you're not a dog, but you still need to come when I call you," I admonished him. "Your little disappearing act took about five years off my life, and that's not very nice at all."

"Mew." I detected a hint of remorse in his reply, so it was okay.

I never did figure out where he was hiding. I told Erica about it that night, and we had a good laugh. It was the next day that she dropped the bomb on me.

"I've got bad news," Erica said, as she unloaded her lunch pail from the day.

"What's up?"

"I found a home for Zoey and Radar."

"But that's great news!" I said. At the same time as I said it, I was horrified to realize that I was a little sad at the idea of them going away. They were just getting into the playful age, and I was starting to have a good time dragging the mouse on a string around for them.

"Okay, I'm a little sad," I admitted. "When are they going?"

"Next weekend." She sounded bummed out, and I decided that if I was a little sad, she was probably devastated. She is a crazy cat lady, after all.

"I'll get you some ice cream," I promised. Ice cream is generally a sure bet to make her happy. "On the upside, the rest of the cats will probably start hanging out with you again!"

She didn't seem very cheered up. When the day came, I will admit that I got a little teary carrying them down the stairs. Somehow, despite the pain, suffering, and lack of sleep, I had managed to get attached to them. Erica is extremely picky about who she will allow adoptees to go to, so I know they ended up in a great home. I think about them once in a while. If I get to missing them too bad, I try to just think about the first week, and look at all the little scars on my hands. That usually takes the sting out of it, at least for a while.

9

Follow The Doc

One of the things I do is make educational videos for the clinic's YouTube page and our website. Some of them are a themed series, like the *Follow the Doc* series, or the *Technician Edition* series, and others are just stand-alone videos. I have learned a lot since I started making these. For example, I've learned that it could take anywhere from twenty minutes to six hours to make a three-minute video. I've also learned that the video that you start out to make might not be the one you end up with.

I went with Dr. Allison and Liz, her technician, to film an episode of *Follow the Doc.* This was going to be about what happens on a Wellness visit. Wellness is an annual program that we offer that covers all of the basic health needs of a horse, like vaccines, a dental float, physical exam, parasite load evaluation, and things like that. I picked this particular trip because they were going to see Tater and Waylon. Tater is a miniature donkey, and Waylon is a miniature horse, and how could you not find such a pair just adorable?

I followed Dr. Allison and Liz out to the farm. Right off the bat, I got some great footage. Tater and Waylon were walking down the fence line, moving towards the same gate we were driving towards. I decided this would be a perfect introduction shot, with the vet truck driving up to the gate, and the little horse and donkey walking over to meet them. I like to do a little intro to my videos with a title screen, some music, and a bit of action like this, another title screen, and then getting into the meat of the video. (Just so you don't get the wrong impression, I learned everything I know about making YouTube videos by watching YouTube videos, so it's not like I'm classically trained or anything.)

After recording the arrival, I drove over and parked beside Dr. Allison. The house, which was a very nice ranch style, was on our right. Someone clearly spent a lot of time manicuring the lawn and shrubs around it, and they were a serious fan of statuary. The barn was on our left. There was no doubt that it was built just for Waylon and Tater, because it was tiny! It looked a lot like a normal barn, with tan walls and brown trim, but it was much smaller.

Once we got to the barn, I confirmed with Wendy, the owner, that it was alright that we film the visit. Wendy was a trip. She was probably around sixty, with salt and pepper hair, an infectious laugh, and she obviously doted on Waylon and Tater.

"We'd like to make an educational video of what a Wellness visit is like," I explained. "That way people who aren't already on Wellness can get a better idea of what it's all about. You've got the two cutest critters in town, and we thought they'd be perfect for the role."

"Oh, I think it's terrific," she said, scratching Tater behind the ears. "They're both such hams, they were born to be entertainers."

"Alright then, let's make them famous!" I laughed.

I carried in the dental box and bucket while Dr. Allison and Liz pulled vaccines and sedation. When everyone was ready, I gave a brief rundown on the plan, since this was Dr. Allison's first time filming one of these with me.

"So, I'd like to get a quick clip of you in front of them, maybe scratching an ear or something, and introduce yourself, introduce the animals, and tell us in a sentence what we're doing here today. Then, you two go to work and pretend like I'm not even here. I'll video most of the process, and then we'll edit it down later, and record you narrating the action. That way you can focus on what you're doing here, rather than thinking about what you're saying. Sound good?"

"So, do we need to be quiet the whole time?" Liz asked.

"Oh no, you can talk," I assured her. "I can eliminate the audio, and we'll dub over it with a scripted narration. You won't hear anything from today except the introduction."

"I should have put on some make-up this morning," Dr. Allison giggled.

She really didn't need make-up. She is one of those naturally pretty people, with light brown hair, rosy cheeks, and eyes that sparkle, but I couldn't come up with a way to explain that to her without making it weird, so I just didn't even try.

"It's dark in this stall," Wendy lamented. "I hope you'll be able to see them on the video."

I took a quick test video, just to see how bad the lighting problem was.

"Oh, we'll be fine," I said. "This thing works wonders in low light. And as long as you stay nervous, your cheeks will be naturally blushed, so it's all working out perfect!"

Liz held the lead ropes, and Dr. Allison took her position. She smoothed her hair, giggled, blushed, and took a deep breath.

"Okay," she said.

I held the camera up, pressed record, and gave her The Nod.

"Does that mean go?" she asked.

I laughed. "Yep, the nod means go. I should have explained that, my bad. We'll do it again."

I reset the camera and gave an exaggerated slow nod. My silliness got the best of me, and I burst out laughing at the same time that she started to speak.

"I'm sorry," I said. "That was terribly unprofessional." I giggled again. "Okay, I think I got it out of my system. Here we go, deep breath in, deep breath out."

We all sighed, I held up the camera, and away we went.

"Hi, I'm Dr. Allison with Springhill Equine. Today we're doing a Wellness visit with Waylon and Tater, two of our cutest clients." She laid it down like a professional that's done it a hundred times.

"Wow, that was perfect!" I said.

"Are you sure?" she asked. "I can make it longer."

"Nope, let's leave it just like that."

"Okay," she agreed. "Let's get to work. Does it matter which one goes first?"

"Not to me," I said.

Waylon was standing closest, so it was decided that he would go first.

"Okay, so we'll do the physical exam first, then we'll sedate him and do the dental, clean his sheath, give vaccines and draw blood for the Coggins test, and take a fecal sample last," she said.

I moved around to the side to get a better angle, and she began the exam. Waylon was a perfect model, standing quietly and lifting his feet up when asked. His bushy mane hung down his neck and covered his eyes, which added significantly to his adorableness, but it made it hard to see a lot of his body from the front. We switched sides, and she examined him from nose to tail.

"Okay," said Dr. Allison. "Let's go ahead and get him sedated for the dental."

There is some pretty impressive math that goes on for this. You have to sedate the horse enough that you can put a speculum on to hold their mouth open, hold their head still, and be able to reach your hand inside their mouth and grind the sharp edges off their teeth with a dental tool without them fighting you, but you don't want to sedate them so much that they can't stand up. It's a very fine balance, and in order to get it right, you need to know how much the horse weighs. A weight tape does a pretty good job of estimating weight based on circumference, and that's a useful tool, as most people don't have a horse-sized scale lying around.

Once Waylon was in the zone, as I call it, they got

started on the dental. Horse dentals are a bit different from people dentals. Their teeth continue to erupt all their life. The constant chewing of grass wears them down, but they don't wear evenly. A ridge forms as a result of the chewing motion not using the entire width of the tooth, and this reduces the efficiency of their chewing. That leads to reduced efficiency in digesting, and essentially the older they get, the less nutrition they get from their food. Regular dentals flatten out the ridges, and keep the efficiency levels high, which helps the horse maintain weight and age better. This tooth wear issue is one of the main reasons that horses in the wild only live fifteen to twenty years, and horses that get regular dental care live from twenty-five to thirty-five years.

Dentals on miniature horses have a different set of challenges than those on full-size horses. Liz held Waylon's head up, and Dr. Allison squatted down as low as she could. Sedated horses can still move, to include jumping and kicking, so it wasn't safe for her to sit on the floor, which would have made this easier. Her headlamp provided all of the illumination inside his mouth, and she had to be able to see what she was doing. To Waylon's credit, he stood still and let them do the work.

I filmed the process from a few different angles. I learned that it's challenging to film a miniature horse getting his teeth done without having someone's butt as a prominent part of the focus. I also learned that when the headlamp is on, it changes the lighting dynamic dramatically! Well, short of going to film school, this is how we learn things. I got some good close-in views that had both good light and no butts, so I felt like we were doing ok. I also planned to have a mix of shots from both animals, so I didn't actually need more than a good minute of dental video.

"Alright," said Dr. Allison, standing up and stretching. "That wasn't too bad."

Liz released the speculum and took it off, and Waylon's head drooped to the floor. His lower lip was loose, which is one of the ways you can tell when they are in the zone. I always have to resist the urge to grab it when it's relaxed like that and do a Mr. Ed impression. Not that anyone knows who Mr. Ed is anymore, but he was a talking horse who had his own sitcom about a hundred years ago. Okay, maybe not a hundred years, but it was in black and white, so, yeah, basically. I give you permission to put the book down for a minute and go find an episode of Mr. Ed on YouTube, but only for familiarization purposes. You can binge watch later.

"Okay, Waylon," Dr. Allison said. "We're going to take a little blood, and give you a couple of shots, right after I clean your sheath. You just stand there and be a good boy." She pulled on a rubber glove, and reached down and pulled out the smegma from his sheath area. This is a goopy combination of skin secretions and dirt that builds up around the retracted penis of horses. It can be a dangerous thing to leave in, as it can cause problems, but it can also be dangerous to take out, as horses don't like you messing with that area, and you can get kicked.

Liz was holding his halter to keep him steady, but he didn't make a move. Dr. Allison pulled off the glove, took the needles from Liz, and quickly gave him the vaccines and drew a vial of blood.

"Oh, I almost forgot," she said. "We need a fecal sample for the egg count." She pulled a plastic bag out of her pocket.

"He pooped right there in the corner just after he walked in here while ago," said Wendy.

"Oh, perfect!" Dr. Allison collected a bit in the baggie, and wrote his name on it with a magic marker.

Next, it was Tater's turn. He had been quietly standing on the other side of the stall watching everything go down. I don't know why I thought he would be as well-behaved a Waylon. Donkeys never are.

I got some decent video of the physical exam, although Tater had no interest in picking up his feet. That involved a lot of shuffling to one side and another, three-legged hopping forward and backward. Liz did her best to hold him still, but a determined donkey is like a bulldozer, even when it's a miniature.

If Tater was disinterested in picking up his feet, then he was actively interested in not getting sedated. It's hard to find the vein on donkeys to begin with, and Tater was not going to take a needle if he could help it. I put the camera away and moved in to help Liz hold him still. After a few strenuous minutes, Dr. Allison sounded the all clear.

"Got it," she said, sounding a little breathless. We backed off to let the sedative take effect.

Within a few minutes, Tater's head was drooping, so we went about the task of getting the speculum on him. As soon as Liz lifted his head, he began backing up. I stepped over to the other side of him, opposite of Liz.

"Let's let him back into the corner," she suggested. "That way we just have to keep him from going three directions, instead of four."

Tater jammed himself into the corner, and we crowded around him. I braced against his side with my legs and tried to hold his head up while Liz braced his other side, holding the speculum as Dr. Allison guided it into place and buckled the strap. Tater twisted his head every which way the entire time.

"You really have to admire his commitment to resistance," I grunted. "It's pretty impressive."

"I'm serious," Liz agreed. "Imagine doing this without sedation!"

"Pass," said Dr. Allison. We all laughed.

She switched on her headlamp and squatted down to take a look in Tater's mouth. Liz lifted his head up, but Tater immediately twisted away. I grabbed the side of the speculum, and she got a better hold on her side, and together we strained to hold him still.

"This is going to be tough," Liz said. "I hope his teeth aren't too bad."

"They're pretty decent," Dr. Allison said, shifting around with his head, trying to keep the light inside his mouth. "It shouldn't take too long, but if he keeps on fighting, we may have to give him a bit more sedation."

Within a minute of trying to start on his teeth, we stopped for more sedation. It was a little easier to give him the shot this time, but only a little. We gave the shot a few minutes to kick in, and then spread the speculum again and got started.

The way it ended up working was Tater stood backed in to the corner, and flat up against one wall. Liz held his head up, while leaning her hip into his shoulder to minimize his forward movement. I stood right behind her, holding him up against the wall as best as I could. Wendy stood behind me, bracing his read end. The five of us shuffled around in a small circle, with Dr. Allison occasionally getting the dental tool on a tooth. We spent about thirty minutes on it, before she announced her satisfaction.

"Ok, I don't think I'm going to get it much better than that," she sighed. "This guy is tough!"

While we still had a hold of him, she gave him his vaccines and pulled blood, and we let him go.

"Well, I don't think we'll be able to feature Tater much in the video," I said. "I didn't actually get any footage after about the first minute."

"Waylon is the cuter one anyway," said Wendy. "Tater is just good comic relief."

I couldn't disagree with that. If you weren't the one trying to hold him still, or the one trying to work on his teeth, the whole thing was probably hilarious. If you happen to watch this video on our YouTube channel, I hope you'll appreciate how it all went down!

10

The Forked Tongue

Part of the identity of our veterinary clinic is that everyone who works there is a horse person. Most of them compete in one thing or another, but some of them just have horses in the back yard. One of the advantages of being a horse person who works at an equine veterinary clinic is that you get a nice discount on your equine healthcare. It's a pretty sweet perk.

Terri, one of our technicians, brought two of her horses into the clinic one Friday. One of them needed a lameness exam to find out why it wasn't moving right. The other one was along for the ride to keep the lame horse company in the trailer, and at the clinic, as they were spending the day there.

One of Erica's superpowers is that she is really good at figuring out things like that. Lameness in horses is not something I ever thought about in my life before I met Erica, as most people probably don't consider such things, but the more I learn about it, the more I realize what a tricky thing it is.

Horses can't tell you where they are sore, so you have to do a bit of reverse cause and effect thinking to follow the trail of clues to figure out where to start looking. In addition to being bad at verbalizing the problem, they also have massively thick muscles. A lot of their torso can't be effectively seen with X-ray or ultrasound. You can't always tell from checking the surface muscles for sensitivity if the muscles underneath them are sore or not. Add in the fact that horses are naturally stoic, and try to hide their pain, and you have a serious challenge.

I don't pretend to know what all goes into a lameness evaluation, so I will suffice to say that they did whatever magic it is that they do, and at the end of the day, Terri loaded up the horses and headed home, which for her was down near Ocala, about an hour drive, pulling the horse trailer.

Erica had just arrived home from work, changed into riding breeches, and was drinking a glass of water when Terri called. I could only hear Erica's side of the conversation, but that was enough to know something wasn't good.

"Hello?"

"Oh my God! How did he manage that?"

"Where are you?"

"Okay, we'll be there in twenty minutes."

I was already putting my shoes on by the time she hung up.

"I've got to put my work clothes back on quick," she said. "This one's going to be bloody."

"What happened?" I asked, following her to the bedroom.

"Terri said she felt a big commotion in the trailer as she was coming into Archer. She pulled over at the feed store to check on the horses, and Mr. Chives had blood pouring out of his mouth. She can't tell if he bit his lip, or his tongue, or what."

We drove to Archer as fast as we could. Terri's truck was in the feed store loading yard, parked up under a tree in the shade. She stood in front of it smoking a cigarette as we pulled in. I drove up right beside the trailer and parked.

Terri is an interesting person. She's a late-fifties Native American horse fanatic who spent half her career as a deputy sheriff, and the other half as an EMT and ambulance driver. I wouldn't say that she is militant about being a lesbian, but she's at least national guard-ish about it, if that makes sense. For example, if you were giving her directions, and you said, "go straight for six miles," she would say "I don't go *straight* anywhere!" She is great fun to hang out with, and super laid back.

"Wow, you made record time," Terri grinned. "I barely had time to call mom and tell her what was going on. I'm supposed to go over to her place and drop off a saddle later."

Terri is not a fast driver. Not at all. Impressing her with your trip time is like impressing a toddler by how strong you are; there just isn't a lot of satisfaction in it. I grinned at her.

"Hey, I take my job as the weekend emergency tech and ambulance driver seriously," I said. "I don't know how you drive this thing in the daytime, but at night, we hustle!"

That was a lie, because Erica has mentioned Terri's slow driving more than once. It's practically lore at the office. She's a great sport about it, partly because she was an actual ambulance driver for so many years, and is enjoying the slower pace of semi-retirement.

Erica climbed in the trailer to take a look, and I followed her. Mr. Chives was leaning against the chest bar with his head down and a slightly glazed look in his eyes. His mouth hung open, and a long red string of bloody drool stretched from his mouth to a puddle on the floor. There was blood all over the floor, as well as some spots here and there on the walls.

"I still haven't figured out what he did, or why," Terri said. "There really isn't much of anything for him to catch his mouth on, so either he was fighting with Pickles and got hurt, or he bit himself somehow."

"Let's get him cleaned up so we can see what we've got," Erica said. "I'm going to sedate him so we can get in his mouth."

"Okay," Terri said. "You want me to unload him, or do you want to do it right here?"

"Let's just leave him right here," Erica said. "He's confined, and he won't have to try to get back in the trailer after we sedate him."

We all climbed back out and went to the vet truck to get the necessary items together. Since Terri was the daytime technician, and this was her horse, I stood back and let her assist Erica. While they drew up some drugs in syringes and dug out the pump, I grabbed a bucket and went in search of water.

By the time I made it back to the trailer, Mr. Chives had been sedated and they were waiting on the drugs to kick in. They had the head loop suspended from the ceiling of the trailer, and once his head was drooping, we lifted it up and rested his chin inside the loop. This kept his mouth at a stable and workable height, and Erica began to flush his mouth out. It already looked like a murder scene inside the trailer, and with the pink, frothy water pouring out the door onto the ground, I was almost nervous about what this must look like to the feed store patrons and staff.

"Damn," Erica said. "It looks like he managed to rip his tongue in half."

She shined her head lamp on his tongue. Now that the gore was washed away, we could see that it was split right up the center for about four inches, starting at the tip. It was the same general shape as a snake tongue, except about a thousand times bigger. I tried to imagine how that could have happened, but I couldn't come up with a plausible scenario.

"What can you do about that?" I asked. It looked pretty hopeless to me, not that I know anything about newly-forked tongues.

"Oh, we'll put some sutures in that and it will heal up like new," Erica said. "It's not near as bad as it looks, and tongues are great at healing fast."

"Well, that's a relief," said Terry. "Mr. Chives can't be down for too long; he's got a hot date at the trail challenge in September."

"He'll be fine by then," Erica assured her. "He's going to need a few weeks off from the bridle, but that's about all."

We climbed back out of the trailer and went over to the vet truck to get everything ready. Terri cleaned up as much of the bloody mess on the floor as she could to give Erica a less-slippery work area. Armed with a local anesthetic for the tongue, sutures, clamps, and towels, we headed back into the trailer. Together, Erica and Terri carefully put the dental speculum on the horse to hold his mouth open during the procedure.

Erica started by giving Mr. Chives a series of shots all around both sides of his tongue to keep him from feeling the needle while she was suturing him up. Next, she dried the tongue off with a clean towel.

"Alright, I'm going to need some extra hands," she announced. "I'm going to put a clamp on each side of his tongue. I need you to hold that side still and centered, and you hold this side still and centered."

We got into position, and Erica put the first clamp in place. It looked like a pair of stainless-steel scissors, except the ends looked like pliers instead of blades, and the handle locked in place when you squeezed them shut. Terri took the clamp, and Erica applied the other one, which I held. She prepared her suture, adjusted her headlamp, and started sewing.

After a few stitches, she stopped and reset the clamps, moving them further down the tongue. It had stopped bleeding, but was fairly swollen. I tried to imagine how it would feel if my tongue were ripped in half like that. The thought made me shiver.

We had to reset the clamps one more time, and then it was done. I fed Pickles a few treats for being so well-behaved while we worked on Mr. Chives. He accepted the treats like a gentleman.

"These are dissolvable stitches," Erica said. "They... why am I telling you this? You already know how this works."

Terri grinned. "Yeah, he'll be fine. I'll keep an eye on them."

"No food tonight, but tomorrow you can ease him onto his regular food," Erica said. "You know the drill."

"I really appreciate you doing this," Terri said. "I hate that I screwed up your Friday night."

"Are you kidding me?" I exclaimed. "What could we have possibly done that would be more exciting than this?"

"As long as I get to ride Ernie at some point this evening, I'm happy too," Erica said. "Although, if you have another revolt in the trailer on the way home, I'll still come sew him up again."

"Oh, there better not be another one of these incidents today," Terri said. "One is the limit!"

We waved as we pulled away. It really was a pretty exciting evening, and it's always good when things end well for everyone involved. After all, that's our whole mission.

11

Big Bouncing Babies

Another early morning phone call: not a great way to get plucked out of a dream, but not as bad as the alarm clock. Being a morning person, I generally wake up on my own before five am, so I don't usually wake up to either sound. This call was not unexpected though. As a matter of fact, it was a day late.

"Hi, Mrs. Cotton," Erica said, rolling over and sitting up on the edge of the bed.

She was silent, listening for a moment, and then confirmed my suspicions. "We'll be there in twenty minutes."

I squinted at the clock on the nightstand, trying to decipher what it was saying: 4:03.

"The Cotton foal is here," Erica said as she got up. "The alarm just went off."

"Well," I said, sitting up, "at least it waited until it was almost time for me to get up, anyway."

The foal alarm is an ingenious invention. Essentially, a small device is stitched in place on the mother horse right where the baby horse is expected to emerge, with a string going from one side to the other. Liquids will pass right over this string, but when a large solid object like a baby horse comes out, it pulls the string out, which activates the tiny transmitter. The transmitter signals the base unit, which is plugged into a phone line, and the base unit calls you and says something to the effect of "Congratulations! You're having a baby!"

One of the other common ways of knowing that a baby horse is being born is the "camp out in the barn and stare at the mother horse" technique. I have not had to do this, for which I am grateful. We do board pregnant mares at the clinic for foal watch, but we have a camera system in the stalls. This way, instead of camping out at the clinic, or waking up every hour and driving over there to check, we just take turns among the staff waking up and checking the cameras on our phone or laptop. You still lose a lot of sleep with this method, but at least it can all happen from the comfort of the bed!

We got dressed quickly and headed north to the Cottons. I was a bit sad that the mare hadn't waited another fifteen minutes. Being a mild tech junkie, and a total caffeine addict, I always set up the coffee pot at night before I go to bed. It turns on automatically at four-fifteen in the morning, and when I wake up, there is a fresh pot of coffee, ready to go. All I have to do is get up and walk in the kitchen and pour a cup. This morning, I was walking out the door nine minutes before it even turned on, and I had no time to wait on it to brew.

The Cottons are a very interesting couple. They are somewhere in their mid-eighties, although that's just a guess. They have a beautiful horse farm on a very scenic, rolling landscape. The region is wooded with lots of live oaks, and the pastures are very green and well taken care of. Everything is bordered in black wooden rail fencing, as is customary on the more well-to-do horse farms. They breed one or two horses a year, and train the young horses, and sell them after a few years.

I drove as fast as I dared. The concern of a speeding ticket was enough to keep me within site of the speed limit, but the fear of hitting a deer was what really kept me from rocketing down the highway. Out in rural places like this, there are all kinds of raccoons, opossums, and armadillos conducting their business on the roads at nighttime. I didn't want to hit any of them, either.

As I pulled into the driveway and stopped at the gate, I saw Mrs. Cotton on the other side of the gate on a golf cart. She opened the gate with a remote control, and then zipped off down the driveway. I followed behind her.

"She's going faster on the golf cart than I feel comfortable going in the truck," I said, as we swung off the paved driveway and headed across the field towards the lighted barn in the distance. "She's going cross country like a baja truck racer."

We bounced along behind her and pulled up near the barn. Mrs. Cotton was already off the golf cart and waiting outside the door before I even got it in park and shut the lights and motor off. She might be elderly, but she doesn't mess around.

"Good morning!" I said with a smile. "I heard you're going to be a new mom!"

"I already am," she said. "The foal hit the ground about five minutes ago. Herbert's over there with them. You grab your stuff and I'll meet you in that pen right there." She pointed beside the barn, and then set off at a fast clip. She was tiny, probably not much more than five feet tall. Arthritis was bending her over in the spine, but it wasn't slowing her down any.

I hurried around the back of the truck, where Erica was getting her stuff together. I grabbed the bucket, which we would put the placenta in so we could check it out later, and a few pairs of disposable rubber gloves. Erica grabbed her stethoscope, thermometer and headlamp, and then we headed towards the pen where Mrs. Cotton had vanished.

The barn lights reached out into the front half of the paddock. Beyond the edge of the light, I could see a flashlight bobbing. My eyes were slowly adjusting to the darkness as we approached, and at last I made out the mare and the foal, both of whom were lying down.

"Howdy," said Mr. Cotton. "They're both lying right where they started out. The foal is about seven minutes now. They both laid flat for a while, but when the baby sat up, she did too." He pointed his flashlight at the foal, but the beam was so weak we couldn't see anything. "My light's dying, so I can't see too much now."

"You couldn't see much if it wasn't dying," said Mrs. Cotton. She turned to us. "He can't see as well since he had his stroke last year, but he won't admit it. Do you want some coffee?"

"Yes ma'am, that would be fantastic," I said. I didn't know if it would be rude to laugh or not, but I couldn't help giggling a little bit at her faux brusque manner.

Mrs. Cotton walked back over to the barn and hopped on the golf cart, which immediately whisked off into the darkness. Erica turned on her headlamp and lit up the scene.

"I can see pretty good with that thing," said Mr. Cotton. "I think I need to trade flashlights with you!"

"Yeah, this thing is pretty fantastic," Erica said. "I couldn't make it without it."

The foal lay behind its mother. The amniotic sack still enveloped its body, but its head and legs were poking through it. The ragged tissue was stretched across the ground, disappearing under the tail of the mare. With the sudden arrival of more visitors, lights and attention, she stood up.

"Easy, momma," said Erica. "Just stand easy."

I moved over to hold on to her halter while Erica listened to her heart.

"Here, let me grab her lead rope," Mr. Cotton said, turning towards the gate.

"Oh no, we shouldn't need it," said Erica. "I just wanted to make sure she's doing okay. We're going to turn her loose here and see if she'll get her baby cleaned up and pass the placenta on her own."

Once Erica was finished, I guided the mare around in a shuffling turn so she was pointed at the foal. As soon as I let her go, she leaned in and began licking her baby.

"There, that's a good girl," Erica murmured. She shut off the head lamp. "Okay, we're going to let her handle it for a bit."

We took a few steps back. The mare continued to nuzzle the baby, licking at the sack and tearing it away a bit at a time. The baby twisted its head around, trying to keep away from the persistent tongue.

A few minutes went by, and my eyes got more accustomed to the darkness. The sky was clear, and we were far enough from town that you could see thousands of brilliant stars on display. As a backyard astronomer, I love standing in a field and looking at the stars. I was basking in the moment, relishing the opportunity to welcome a new life, and to be able to look out on the beautiful galaxy at the same time, when a sudden husking sound behind me made my heart miss a few beats.

I spun around, trying to identify the sound. I was sure that I was about to be killed by some terrible unknown, when the sound happened again. I looked closer, and made out the shape of a tree I hadn't noticed earlier. It clicked for me then, that the sound I was hearing were the claws of an animal, or more than one, racing up the side of the tree. As I stared at the tree, I heard the sound again, and this time I saw a blur come racing down the trunk, with another one right behind it. They raced straight towards me, and I dropped into a crouch, still not exactly sure what I was dealing with. Just before they got to me, the one in front spun around and leaped into the air, landing on top of the one behind it.

"Peanut Butter and Jelly!" Erica cried, snapping on her light again.

In the sudden glare of the bright light, two cats crouched. One was calico, and the other one was gray. They weren't really big, but they had a ton of hair, and it stuck straight out, making them seem twice the size they really were. Erica ran over and gathered them up in her arms, covering them in smooches and subjecting them to a minute of corporal cuddling. I relaxed my defensive posture.

"So, this is the infamous duo," I said. "I've heard all kinds of stories about them."

"Yep, this is Peanut Butter," said Erica, gesturing with an elbow, "and this is Jelly. Aren't they just the cutest things you ever saw?" She sat them down, and they immediately raced away and jumped up on the top rail of the fence, near the barn. Silhouetted in the light from the barn like that, they looked like a surreal scene from a movie. I couldn't help but laugh as they chased each other up and down the fence.

"They certainly know how to have a good time," I said.

"Oh, those two are a handful," Mr. Cotton said. "You can't do anything without them being in the middle of it."

As we watched them, a tiny pair of headlights appeared, and a moment later, Mrs. Cotton whipped up to the gate. I went over and opened the gate, and she came in carrying four big insulated coffee mugs.

"Wow, how did you manage to carry all those and drive at the same time?" I asked.

"Oh, this isn't my first baby," she said with a laugh. "I've hauled enough food and coffee down here to the barn over the years to feed an army."

I believed her. Every time I met Mrs. Cotton, I got the impression that despite being slight in stature, she was very capable of handling anything and everything, and she was unquestionably in charge. I took two of the cups from her after I latched the gate.

"The one in your left hand has creamer, and goes to Erica," she said. "The other one is black, for you."

"Thank you," Erica said. "Kittens and coffee, you know how to make me happy!"

We all sipped our coffee quietly for a few minutes. The kittens raced around in the darkness nearby, engaging in epic battles, followed by fence races, followed by brief stops near the people to get some attention.

Erica turned the light back on to check the mare's progress. The foal was completely out of the sack by now, and looked considerably better after its bath. It was dark brown, with a white blaze on its head, and a white sock on its right rear leg. It turned its eyes away from the light, and with a sudden burst of activity, thrust its front legs out, and began rocking forward. Its back legs scrabbled for purchase, sliding sideways across the dew-soaked grass. Finally, one of its tiny hooves caught, and it lurched up. Unfortunately, it didn't get the other back leg into position, and it crashed back down.

"Oh, that was a good try," Erica said. "Take a second to rest, and we'll try it again."

The foal lunged again, pushing with all four legs in wild directions. Erica held its back end up as it leaned over, and steadied it as it finally achieved a standing posture.

"Twenty-eight minutes," Mr. Cotton announced. "Standing in twenty-eight minutes, that's pretty good."

While she had a hand on the foal, she raised the tail and took a quick temperature reading. "It's a boy," she called.

"A colt, eh," Mrs. Cotton grunted. "That seems to be the streak we're on. We've had three colts out of this mare now, and the first two did really good."

"She puts out a nice foal," Erica agreed. "This one looks to have the same coloring as the last one did, except with just the one white sock."

She stepped back to give the foal some space. He wobbled around a bit, trying to get the hang of holding his head up and his legs down. He took a tentative step forward, wobbled precariously, caught himself, wobbled again, and fell down. Peanut Butter and Jelly raced over and pounced on him.

"Hey, get on, now," cried Mr. Cotton, shooing them away. "Go play in the barn!"

I was in the middle of taking a drink at that very moment, and I almost snorted coffee out my nose; it was a very near thing. I managed to swallow it at last, but not before my eyes teared up. My chest was hitching as my body kept trying to send the coffee in my mouth someplace, whether it was out my nose, or back out my mouth to the ground, or down my throat. Once I managed to swallow, I coughed for a few minutes. Erica handed me a rag so I could clean myself up and try to regain my dignity.

The kittens raced away, leaping back on to the fence near the gate. I blew my nose and shook my head, waiting for the burning sensation to recede.

"Caught you at a bad time, huh?" Mrs. Cotton chuckled. "Those cats are cute as a button, but they cause more trouble than I can keep up with."

"I think I'm okay," I said. "I certainly wasn't expecting them to jump on the foal. That was hilarious." I wiped my eyes.

During the commotion, the foal had managed to get to his feet again, unassisted this time. He took a step towards the mare, who leaned down and began licking him clean again.

"Next comes the frustrating part," Erica said to me. This was my first time at the actual foaling, so I hadn't experienced the stuff that happens in the first few hours. "He's going to want to nurse here pretty soon, but he's going to have a really hard time finding the nipple. It's tough to watch, because you want to help them, guide them to it, but you can't. If you try to push his head, he'll pull it the other way. If you try to reverse-psychology him, he'll still go the wrong way."

"Yep," Mrs. Cotton confirmed. "I've had a lot of foals in my life, and I can tell you, you just gotta let 'em find it. They get so close, then they start going to other way, and you just want to tell them 'go back, go back!' It's painful to watch them get so close, and then go to the whole other end of their momma."

They weren't wrong. The foal was soon running his muzzle around his mother, nipping and pulling here and there. I tried to think of something to compare it to, and the best thing I could come up with was watching a four-year-old kid play miniature golf. To complicate matters, the mare was growing restless. Just as the foal would seem to be making some progress and start getting close to the udder, she would take a step or two away, flicking her tail and tossing her head. Then we would start all over again.

At last, a brief transfer of milk took place. I think it sort of happened by accident, as it took a few minutes for him to get it a second time, but we all cheered anyway.

"It's about time," said Mr. Cotton. "You just about ran yourself out of energy looking for the food!"

Now that it had had a taste, the sense of urgency was redoubled. The foal went after it in earnest, pulling at the udder and the skin around it repeatedly, causing the poor mare to twitch, until it finally managed to latch on a second time. After nursing for a few minutes, the foal stepped back, licked his lips, and flopped own.

"Nap time!" said Mrs. Cotton.

The mare laid down a moment later. She still had not passed the placenta.

"Is that a big deal?" I asked, pointing at it.

"Not yet," Erica said. "The rule of one, two, three gives her three hours to pass the placenta. It's only been about an hour and a half so far."

The sun was trying to break the horizon. The stars were starting to disappear, and the birds were waking up. I finished my coffee, grateful to have it.

"So, one hour to stand, and two hours to nurse, right?" I asked.

"Right," Erica said.

"I know you've told me this stuff before," I said as an apology, "but you've told me a lot of horse stuff, and my retention doesn't start getting decent until the third or fourth repetition."

"Don't beat yourself up," said Mr. Cotton. "Right about the time you manage to retain everything you learned, you start forgetting it due to old age. You can't win."

"That's exactly how it's going to happen for me," I laughed. "I got a late start on learning this stuff, so the deck is already stacked against me."

The foal napped for about fifteen minutes, and was up on his feet again, looking much more solid and a lot less wobbly. He nursed again for a moment, and then took a step back. He stood very still, and his little tail raised up in the air. He braced his legs in a wide stance, and stood still again, his head cocked slightly.

"Alright," said Erica. "This is another one of those moments we were waiting for: the meconium. It's basically a seal that keeps the fluids out while he's in the womb, and I like to make sure they pass it so they don't get bound up right off the bat."

The foal completed his first poop, which wasn't actually poop, but I was still impressed. He had done more in the first two hours of his life than human kids do in nine months.

"It's amazing how fast the prey species develop mobility," I said. "Even though I know this is how it works on an intellectual level, it still blows my mind to watch it happen."

"Yep, it's always amazing to see," Mrs. Cotton agreed. "I never get tired of watching the new ones in their first few weeks. It's more than just being cute. It's a miracle of nature happening that you get to see."

"We are fortunate people," I said.

"Yes, we are," Mrs. Cotton said. "Yes, we are."

She gathered up the coffee cups. "I'm going up to the house for a minute," she said. "Does anyone want more coffee?"

We all declined, and a moment later she was cruising up the hill on the golf cart.

"She sure gets around on that thing," I chuckled.

"Oh, yes," said Mr. Cotton. "She runs the wheels off of that cart."

The mare passed the placenta just then, and it hit the ground with a plop. I grabbed the bucket and a pair of gloves and walked over with Erica.

"Let's put it in the bucket and take it over to the barn aisle so we can see it clearly," Erica said. We carefully put it in the bucket and walked over to the gate. "Grab the hose and let's rinse it off."

I grabbed the hose and turned the water on. Erica lifted the placenta out of the bucket and carefully rinsed it off. Peanut Butter and Jelly came out of nowhere, sniffing the water, the bucket, and the placenta itself. I shooed them away, but it didn't do any good.

"I'll hold them, if you'll hand them to me," said Mr. Cotton. "By the time I get bent over to pick them up, they've moved out of reach."

I laughed, and grabbed them up and handed them to him. Erica finished rinsing the placenta, and I shut the hose off while she stretched it out, looking for any tears or signs of infection or problems with it that might be an indication of a problem with the foal, and also to make sure that the whole thing came out and didn't leave anything inside the mare. Satisfied, she put it back in the bucket.

"If you'll dump that in that bucket in the tack room, I'll have Robert bury it when he gets here this afternoon," said Mr. Cotton. The kittens squirmed in his arms, attempting to wrestle with each other.

We cleaned everything up and made our preparations to leave.

"I think you've got a healthy baby," Erica said. "I'll be back this afternoon to peek at him, but I think he's all set for right now."

"Yep, he looks good," Mr. Cotton agreed. Jelly got loose and ran up his shoulder, around the back of his head, and down the other arm to attack Peanut Butter. He let them drop to the ground, and they abandoned the fight in favor of licking the blood spots off the concrete that we missed when we sprayed the floor off.

"I'm going to head home and feed my guys," Erica said. "If anything comes up before I get back, give me a call."

"Thanks for getting here so quick this morning," he

said. "We really appreciate you, and the way you take care of things."

"Aww, I never miss a chance to come play with your kittens," she laughed. "But thanks for saying so. I'll see you this afternoon."

We made our way down the driveway. On the way back, Erica surprised me with some client trivia.

"Did you know that he's not Mr.?" she asked.

"What do you mean?"

"He's Dr. Cotton. He was an OB/GYN forever. He probably delivered half the people in this county."

"How about that," I mused. "I guess he never got tired of it; he's still seeing ladies through pregnancies."

Somehow, we were home in time to feed our crew and eat breakfast, and still be right on schedule. It's amazing how much you can get done in a day when you get a good early start.

12

Vacation

It's important to get a change of scenery once in a while, both for your own peace of mind, and for those around you. Absence makes the heart grow fonder, right? Right. So, in that spirit, Erica and I packed up the motorcycle and headed to the mountains of North Carolina for a nice long weekend. We left on a Wednesday morning. Does that count as being a weekend? I don't know, but we counted it.

Some friends of ours own a cabin outside of Murphy, North Carolina, and they offered it to us as a free place to stay in exchange for us looking it over, as they hadn't been up to it in a few months. We didn't know anything about it, other than the address, and I determined that the Google

Maps Street View car had not yet made it to the road the cabin was on. Adventure!

Erica is obsessed with several things, including cats and horses, but one of her more useful obsessions is checking the weather. She has a variety of reasons for this. She works outside, so there is a personal investment in knowing what to wear, and what to expect. If it's going to be cold overnight, the horses may need to have sheets on, or blankets, or both. The horses that compete in show jumping get clipped, so they don't have a winter coat like the retirees. For the purposes of a motorcycle trip, having someone with up-to-the-minute radar information can keep you from riding into a rainstorm.

As we rode down the driveway, leaving on the much-anticipated trip, I tried to think of all the things we might have forgotten to do or pack.

"Did you make sure there was plenty of cat food in the can?" I asked. We have Bluetooth headsets in our helmets, so we can talk while we are riding.

"Yep."

"Did you check the forecast this morning?"

"Yep. Still clear, no chance of rain anywhere in the southeast US for the next week."

"Sweet!" I was very excited to be taking Erica on a five-day motorcycle trip. This was our longest trip yet, as a couple.

Riding a motorcycle across the country is very different than driving a car. For one thing, you are very much at the mercy of the elements. Sunshine, windburn, temperature variations, and rain are all very important factors on a motorcycle that are not really important in a car. Safety is another big difference. There is no such thing as a fender-bender on a motorcycle. Comfort is a factor if you are riding more than a few hours. In a car, you can stretch, shift positions, move your hands to different places on the steering wheel, and so on. On a motorcycle, you can't move much, and you get stiff and sore, even on a luxury touring bike like our Honda Goldwing.

Our goal was to maximize our time spent in the mountains, and minimize the time spent getting there and back, so we took Interstate 75 from Gainesville, Florida up to Atlanta, Georgia, where we changed highways and made our way into the mountain country. We had to stop for fuel and a stretching walk break every two and a half hours or so. On our second stop, just south of Atlanta, Erica checked the weather, and frowned.

"Huh," she said. I could sense something negative in her presentation of the grunt.

"What's up?" I asked.

"There's a storm in South Carolina that wasn't there last time we stopped. It's big, goes all the way out into the Atlantic."

"Huh," I replied. "I guess WeatherBug changed their mind."

"No, they still say no rain," she said.

"They're in denial," I said. "Nobody likes being wrong."

"Well, we'll keep an eye on it," she said, putting the phone away and slipping her helmet on. "It's sort of going the same place we are."

We made it through Atlanta without incident, which is always a death-defying test of nerves and chutzpah. I developed a healthy distaste for Atlanta traffic and the whole I-285 loop back in my days as a truck driver. Going through there on a motorcycle is more dangerous than in a big truck, but you have a lot more mobility. One thing that makes it a little better is that motorcycles are allowed to ride in the HOV lanes, which are generally less hectic, and you only have people trying to kill you from one side instead of two.

We arrived in Murphy about four o'clock that afternoon. Erica pulled out the directions to the cabin, and we headed out of town to find it and get settled in before going back to town for supper. The GPS was useless, as it spent most of the time searching for a signal.

"Okay, there's the school up there on the left, with a blue roof," she said. "We should be turning right on the second road on the right past the school."

I slowed down, watching carefully. The sun was already sinking down near the tops of the mountains, and I couldn't see as well as I would have liked.

"There it is," I said. "So far, so good."

The road was asphalt, but narrow. Two cars passing each other would have to slow down and put their outside tires in the grass to get by. It went straight back, and then climbed the side of the mountain. I don't mean it zig-zagged up the side of the mountain in a series of sensible switchbacks, either. It went straight up the side to the top. I have never seen such a steep road, and I lived in Wyoming at one time!

I climbed it in second gear, leaning forward and praying that my hand didn't twitch on the throttle and cause us to pop a wheelie and flip over backwards.

"I really don't like this road, I really hate this road," I muttered, repeating myself a few times.

Finally, we got to the top of the mountain. I jammed on the brakes and stared in horror at the scene before me.

"Oh my God," I breathed. My heart was jackhammering

in my chest, and I realized that I was white-knuckle gripping the handlebars. I put the transmission in neutral, put the kickstand down, and shut off the bike.

The pavement ended at the top of the mountain about three feet in front of us. From there down the other side, and turning out of sight, the road was gravel. Some motorcycles can handle gravel, like dirt bikes and enduro bikes. Big, heavy cruisers and touring bikes, like the Goldwing, do not handle well in gravel at all. The Goldwing weighs about a thousand pounds, plus two passengers, and it likes to slide out from under you on anything soft. We climbed off the bike to assess the situation.

"Let's walk down and see if we can find the cabin," I suggested. "Maybe we can just leave the bike parked here at night."

Erica gave me a doubtful look, but didn't say anything. We began walking down the road. The part where the tire tracks were was fairly well packed, but there were a lot of washouts going off the sides of the road from rainstorms. Those worried me a little bit.

We rounded the curve, and I saw that the road dropped down more, turning back to the left and going out of site again. We continued on. Around the next bend, the trees opened up. We could see several cabins nearby. We could also see that a small stream crossed the road at the bottom, and that the road went up the side of another mountain, just as steep and straight as the first one.

"This is not good," I said. "What's our address?"

"I think part of the road is paved up there," Erica said hopefully. "We're looking for twenty-nine. That mailbox there says four, so it must be on up the other side."

I looked up the road in the deepening dusk. It did

appear to become paved again partway up. I tried to shake the feeling of dread from my stomach.

"If we walk all the way to the cabin, it's going to be full dark before we get back to the bike," I said. "I really, really don't want to try to negotiate this in the dark."

"Ok," Erica said. "This seems to be pretty solid. I think you'll be fine. It's not near as bad as a dirt road that's under construction, with six inches of soft dirt."

She was referring to our driveway. Twice now, we have gone out for a Sunday ride, and returned to find that the neighbor was working on it with his tractor, and we had to make our way through a mess. On both of those occasions, I very nearly dropped the bike.

"Good point," I said. "Thank you for trying to bolster my confidence."

We walked back to the bike, put our helmets on, and remounted.

"Okay, just as a refresher: if we start to go down, keep your feet on the foot boards, and squeeze with your knees. The crash bars will keep your legs from getting pinned. Just hold on to your handles on the sides of the seat. Don't wiggle, or scoot around, or lean. This is going to be tough enough as it is." I started forward.

"Okay," Erica said. "I got it. And I got you, and you are awesome."

"Thank you, baby," I said. "I'm going to do my best to not let you down." I thought about what I had just said. "I mean that figuratively and literally," I added.

I shifted into second so that the throttle wouldn't be so touchy, and rode the rear brake. We inched down the mountain, and I counted each washout as a victory moment when we crossed them. At last we reached the bottom, which was getting darker by the minute.

"Ok, I can't stop while we're going up the side of this thing," I said. "You're going to have to watch the mailboxes, and try to give me a heads up in case I don't see it."

"Got it," she confirmed. "It ought to be on the right, since all the odd numbers seem to be on the right so far."

We began our ascent. I kept it in first gear this time, so that I wouldn't be carrying too much speed to make a sudden turn into the driveway. I switched the headlights to bright, trying to give us every advantage. Erica called out the mailbox numbers as we approached them.

"Twenty-one."

"Twenty-five."

I maintained speed. The road was just as steep as the first climb we made. We were back on pavement at this point, and I felt a little more confident about veering off the road.

"There's no mailbox on that road," she said. We passed it and continued on.

Suddenly, I realized that the pavement ended ahead, returning to gravel. I gripped the handlebars even tighter, tense from head to toe and unable to relax. We bounced back on to the gravel. The road was so steep I was terrified both of spinning the rear tire in the gravel, which would slide us sideways and over, and of popping a wheelie. I had no idea how much of a possibility either danger was, but from my position, we seemed to be on the cusp of both simultaneously.

"Another one with no mailbox," Erica announced.

"Thirty-five," I read on the next box. "Shit, that means it was one of the ones we passed. I can't stop here, there's no way to turn around. We're just going to have to go to the top."

"Ok, no worries," Erica attempted to soothe me.

The gravel on this end of the road was much looser. It was obvious that it didn't get much traffic. We crested the ridge, and the road turned sharply to the right, and then ended in front of a cabin. I was even more afraid of stopping here, as the gravel was completely loose, and I knew that getting the bike turned around was going to be a nightmare. I stopped, feeling like the hurdles just kept on coming, and I was bound to trip over one eventually.

"Okay, new plan," I said. "Hop off, and let's walk back down and figure out which one it was. I'm not leaving anything else to chance."

"I'm hoping it was the one on the pavement," she said, climbing off the bike.

"Me too, but I'm not holding my breath," I said, grimly.

I shut the engine off and put the kickstand down, and eased the bike over onto it, making sure it wasn't going to sink too far into the gravel to stay upright. Once I was satisfied that it was safe, I got off and we began walking back down the road.

We approached the first driveway, the one that was still on the gravel portion of the road. Erica walked ahead, and called back as she neared the cabin.

"This is it."

I looked at the driveway. Coming from this side, the road was going down at an impossible angle. The driveway was about a sixty degree turn to the left, and it angled up steeply for about twenty feet, where it leveled off into a parking place beside the porch. Getting in was going to be hell, and getting back out was going to be even worse, because the turn downhill was going to be about a hundred and twenty degrees, which is crazy sharp in loose gravel on the side of a mountain. I took a few deep breaths.

"Alright, you stay here," I said. "I'm probably going to crash, either up there at the top, or turning into the driveway here. There's no reason for you to be on the bike for that."

"My helmet is up there," she said. "I've got to go get it, and if you do crash, you'll need me to help you pick the bike up."

She had me cornered with that one.

"I can't argue with your logic," I said, after a moment. "But you're still walking back down." I was actually a bit relieved. She's a wonderfully calming presence when I'm stressed out.

At the top, I did a slow, ten-point turn until I was pointed back down the road. I have never fully appreciated having reverse on a motorcycle the way I did right then. Instead of trying to push the bike backwards in the loose gravel, I was able to use my feet to balance while it pulled itself back. At last, I was ready for the final leg. Erica put her helmet on so we could talk over the headsets if we needed to on the way down.

I eased forward and nosed around the corner. The road fell away before me into the darkness below, as the bike was still fairly level, and the headlights were shining out into space. That was nerve-wracking as hell, so I kept moving to avoid psyching myself out. I kept the bike in first gear, and the engine helped brake the speed. Erica walked behind me, and told me what an impressive job I was doing.

"I think I could have ridden down," she said. "You look like you're just cruising down the road."

"I'm trying to wear a brave face," I replied. "I want to impress you with my hot rod driving skills and my cabin on top of Mount Everest."

"Oh, I'm impressed, alright."

The driveway was coming up. I inched over to the right side of the road so that I would have as much room as possible to get straight before I went from the down-straight angle of the road to the left turn going up and sloping-right angle of the driveway. There was going to be a moment when the back tire was on the road, and the front tire was going up the driveway, and my feet would be well over a foot off the ground. All on loose gravel, mind you. I would be at my most vulnerable at that point. No pressure, right?

"There're probably only three or four people in the world who could make this turn on a Goldwing," I said. "Not that I'm bragging, since I haven't actually done it yet. I'm just saying that this whole road is probably a difficulty level of about thirty-eight."

"What's the range of the difficulty scale?" Erica asked.

"One to ten," I said.

I was at the driveway, so I stopped talking and focused. As I started turning to the left, the front wheel slid for a fraction of a second, and then it recovered its grip. I focused intently on trying to keep my bearings on which way was straight up as I leaned over. It was hard to do on the side of a mountain, especially since it was almost full dark. The ground was much closer to me on the left side than the right, and I fought off the feeling of disorientation. The front wheel left the road and started up the driveway, and I gritted my teeth and focused on my angle and speed, ignoring the fact that I could no longer reach the ground with my feet. At last, the rear wheel joined the front wheel on the driveway, and we climbed to the top and stopped in the semi-level parking area. I sat on the bike for a moment, shaking like a leaf, and thinking about how grateful I was to be there, undamaged.

"Nothing to it," Erica said cheerfully. "Since you're all practiced up now, you want to run into town and get us some supper while I unpack?"

"Oh shit!" I cried in dismay. "I forgot all about food!" I clapped my hand to my forehead, forgetting that I was still wearing my helmet.

"I'm kidding, I'm kidding," Erica laughed. "I'm sure we can find something to eat in the cabin, and we've got a third of a loaf of homemade bread with us. We'll survive until morning."

We unloaded the bike and climbed up the porch steps, physically and mentally exhausted from the day. The Atlanta traffic seemed like weeks ago, not hours. Erica unlocked the door, turned on the lights, and we went in.

It was a huge cabin, one of those two-story places with a deck all the way around the lower level, and glass windows covering the whole front wall looking out over what we assumed was the valley. The bedrooms were upstairs, and I carried the bags up while Erica assessed the kitchen and food situation.

"Well," she called out. "We have, in addition to the bread we brought, one can of tomato soup, and one can of cream of broccoli soup."

"I'll take the soup," I called back down. "It sounds lovely. Can it be served in the shower?"

"It can, but it'll have to wait," she replied. "The water heater has to be turned on in the breaker box, and it's going to take a bit to heat up."

"Supper it is," I said.

She found some bowls and heated the soup in the

microwave. We split the bread and tried not to devour it all too quickly.

"Oh my God, I'm starving," Erica mumbled, blowing on a spoonful of tomato soup. "My hands are shaking."

"Well, you can't say I don't provide an adventure," I said. "Day One: Atlanta traffic, four near death experiences, off-roading on a highway bike, romantic soup dinner, and a cool shower. What more could we have packed into a day?"

"I don't guess I mentioned to Betty that we were going to be on a motorcycle," Erica said. "I think they would have warned me about the road if they had realized that."

"Well, they aren't motorcycle people," I said. "Even if you had mentioned it, it might not have occurred to them that it would be a concern."

"True," she said. "Thanks for not being mad at me about it."

"How could you have known it would be like that?" I said. "Besides, assuming I don't crash in the morning, and even if I do, I guess, we'll have stories to tell about this forever!"

We finished eating, fighting off the exhaustion that was quickly consuming our remaining energy.

"I have zero cell signal," Erica said, after we had cleaned up our dishes.

"It's good for you," I said. "That's Verizon trying to help you be on vacation."

"Uh huh."

When the water was hot, I soaked my aching body in a long, steamy shower, and then slept like the dead. It occurred to me as I was drifting off that there was no coffee for tomorrow morning, but there wasn't anything I could do about that.

The next day, we rode back out. In the daylight, and

being well-rested as opposed to exhausted, the road was slightly less terrifying, though still extremely challenging. We made it around the sharp, angled turn from the driveway onto the road, which was the worst part. After that, I felt better, and we made it out to the highway without any drama. We found a diner in Murphy, and stopped to eat breakfast, drink coffee, and make a plan.

"Hey, I've got a signal," Erica said. As if to confirm that, her phone began chirping incessantly as it downloaded all the missed text messages, calls and voicemails.

I looked at my phone. No missed calls, no text messages. I smiled, and enjoyed my coffee as Erica checked in with the world back home. One of the responsibilities that comes with owning a business, and being connected with clients the way Erica is, is that you have to stay in touch with people, even on vacation. She answered a few messages and emails, and called the office to check in there. I looked at the map on my phone, trying to decide where to go.

After breakfast, when she was all caught up, Erica checked the radar.

"Wow," she said, showing me the phone. "I guess that storm that wasn't supposed to exist hasn't gone away."

The radar showed a massive storm at the north end of Georgia, covering South Carolina, and most of North Carolina, and we were right on the edge of it. I looked outside and studied the sky. It was overcast, but not exactly looking like rain was imminent. By the time we finished our coffee, however, it was sprinkling.

"Well, that creates a dilemma," I said. "There's no way I'm riding the bike back to the cabin in the rain. It's bad enough when it's dry."

"Yeah, that's a problem," Erica agreed. "Especially since we left our stuff there."

We thought about it in silence for a minute.

"Ok, I think we have to change the plan," I said. "That cloud on the radar says it's going to start pouring at some point, and it isn't going to stop. That means staying at the cabin is basically out of the question. Agreed?"

"Agreed," she replied.

"I propose we go back, park at the top of the first hill like we did last night, and walk in and get our stuff. Then we head west, and try to get out in front of this storm that has zero chance of happening, according to the weatherman."

"Deal," said Erica. "Maybe we can drop back down into Georgia and check out some of those state parks you're always telling me about."

By the time we got the cabin cleaned out and the bike packed up, it was pouring rain. We put on our rain suits and headed west. Fortunately, we were still on the edge of the storm, and we managed to ride out of it after a few hours.

"The radar projections show it moving northwest," said Erica. "It doesn't look like it will touch the western side of Georgia. Maybe we can head for Cloudland Canyon?"

"That sounds good," I said. "You'll love it there, it's absolutely fantastic!"

We rode across north Georgia, passing a few places that I really wanted to stop and show Erica, but I was afraid the storm would catch right back up to us if we did. I pointed them out as we passed.

"These are all places that we're going to have to come back and see," I said. "One of these days we'll make a waterfall tour of North Georgia."

"Waterfalls and sunshine tour," she amended. "Sunshine is important."

"Agreed."

We arrived at Cloudland Canyon just after noon. We went into town to eat lunch before heading out to the park. As we waited on the food to come to the table, Erica checked the radar again.

"You're not going to believe this," she said.

"Oh, I might," I replied, pointing behind her. "The Weather Channel is doing a feature on it right now."

We watched together as the meteorologist explained that the Carolinas were experiencing a thousand-year rain event, with unprecedented flooding. The map he showed included our current location in the danger area for the next day.

"We're making this happen," I said. "It's following us. If you'll recall, the forecast yesterday morning was absolutely clear for all of this area. A thousand-year rain event? From out of nowhere? Too suspicious. And the path keeps spreading and changing. It's following us."

"I think you're right," Erica said. "Now what? I really don't want to head back to Florida yet, it's only Thursday."

"Well, I think we have time to see a bit of the park this afternoon," I said. "We can stay here tonight, and head into Alabama tomorrow. Either we'll find a new adventure over there, or we'll make it rain, or both. Maybe we'll just keep going, and drag the rain across the country."

"Hey, there's an idea," Erica said, brightening up a little. "We can sell our rain-making abilities to California! They're having a drought, right? We'll ride the motorcycle to California for ten thousand dollars."

We spent the afternoon hiking in the canyon. Having

been there before, I guided us towards a waterfall that was both breathtakingly spectacular, and close enough that we could get there and back in four hours. The trail worked its way from the rim all the way down to the bottom, and then followed a trickling stream up the canyon floor. We heard the falls long before we could see them. At last, we turned a slight corner, and there it was.

"I know this place!" Erica gasped. "This is from the picture of you on eHarmony!"

I grinned, elated that she recognized it. It wasn't a tall waterfall, but it poured over a shelf and fell about twenty feet into a large pool. The walls of the pool were a very interesting pattern of sediment layers, and wrapped around the pool in a near-perfect semi-circle. In the picture she was referring to, I was tilting my head back in a side profile with my mouth wide open, and my buddy Tom positioned the camera such that it looked like the waterfall was pouring in my mouth. Fun with photography!

"Yep, this is the place," I confirmed. "I knew you'd like it!"

"The whole canyon is unbelievable," she said. "But this picture was one of the reasons I decided I liked you. It showed me that you were adventurous and funny."

We poked around the waterfall for a bit, taking pictures and just soaking up the raw, natural energy. If you ask me, there is nothing like a waterfall to refresh your spirit. With some reluctance, we made the hike back up to the rim, and rode to town to find a motel.

The next morning, it was raining when we awoke. The storm had moved faster than it was supposed to, much to the surprise of no one in our party. We ate breakfast at the hotel, and decided to take the interstate into Alabama, and then beeline south. The idea was that if we put one hundred miles between us and the storm, maybe we could relax and have a stress-free Saturday and Sunday. Going south would put us closer to home too, so that would free up some of Sunday's travel time.

We rode in some pretty serious rain for a few hours, but it got lighter the further we went. Fortunately, traffic was pretty light. There are a variety of dangers associated with riding in the rain, one of which is that you become even more invisible to people in cars and trucks. The more crowded the road, the more dangerous it is to be on a motorcycle. The other danger that keeps me tense is hydroplaning. It's one thing to do it in a car. It's another thing to do it on two wheels!

By the time we were down in central Alabama, we were back in the sunshine. We cut back over into Georgia near Columbus, and visited some Indian Mounds, which were very cool, and then we went to Providence Canyon and hiked around it. That was a very insightful stop, as we learned that this whole amazing little canyon system was the result of bad farming practices and erosion. It was all a field, with trees and grass at one point, and then in the 1800's, people cleared the land and plowed it, and the rain washed down the furrows and cut into the softer, unstable soil beneath, and over time, the furrows became trenches, which became ravines, which became canyons. It's still growing to this day.

On Saturday we rode back into Florida. We went over near Tallahassee and checked out some of the springs there. We got to see some manatees, which was pretty cool. We had a leisurely ride back home afterwards. We didn't end up going anywhere that we had planned to go, but we still made it into an adventure and made the best of things. That's an important part of adventuring. It's also an important part of sharing your life with someone, and I'm glad I've got someone who understands that. Despite the rain, and the insane road to the cabin, and the storm that chased us for three hundred miles, we still had a great time, and that's what it's all about.

13

Hurricane Preparedness

In the previous chapter of my life, sort of my 'dark ages' if you will, before I met Erica, I lived in coastal Georgia with my dog, Angus. Angus has since gone on to chase squirrels in the sky, but for a number of years, it was just the two of us holding the fort down.

Angus and I weathered our share of storms. Even though we never got a direct hit from a hurricane in the twenty-ish years that I lived in coastal Georgia (Hurricane Michael has since broken that streak), we had several serious threats, and being a former Boy Scout, I usually tried to be ready for it. At that time, my preparations consisted of filling the bathtub up with water so I could flush the toilet, filling up a clean thirty-gallon trashcan with water for Angus, making sure there was an abundance of canned goods in the pantry, and filling up some jugs of water for drinking. All told, back then it probably took me thirty minutes to do storm prep.

Recently, Tropical Storm Hermine came across Florida, and I got to experience my first storm prep down here. I will admit that I went into it a little over-confident, and a little underprepared. It never occurred to me until it was time to get ready how different storm preparedness is on a horse farm and at a business. I realized pretty fast that I needed to hustle, because I wasn't going to get it all done in a half hour.

The first problem I had to tackle was water. We get our water from a well, so if the power goes out, the water goes out, too. I really wasn't sure how much water I needed to have on hand, so I asked Erica about it.

"Hey, how much water does a horse drink in a day?"

"On average, about fifteen gallons," she said.

I did some quick math in my head. Six horses and two donkeys times fifteen gallons each equals one hundred and twenty gallons of water per day that I needed to be able to provide if the power went out.

"Has the power ever gone out here for a long period of time? I asked.

"Yeah, a few times," Erica said. "The problem with living out here in the boonies is that there are only six houses on our power line. In an event like a hurricane, we're at the bottom of the priority list for getting power restored. During the last hurricane, we had a tree fall on the line about halfway up the road, and it took them about four days to get it fixed."

I did some more math in my head. I decided I should go through it out loud so Erica could check my work.

"Okay, so we've got five automatic water buckets in the pastures, and they hold about twenty gallons each," I said. "That's a hundred gallons. We've got a five-gallon bucket in each stall, so that's another twenty-five gallons. So that means that if the power goes out, we'll have enough water on hand to make it twenty-four hours or so, not counting any extra water that we put up. Does that sound right?"

"Sounds right," she agreed. "Now keep in mind, not all of them are going to drink a full fifteen gallons every day. Sydney and Gigi are pretty low consumers, and the donkeys aren't going to drink that much."

"Okay, but erring on the side of caution, I'll use that figure as a goal," I said. "That way I've got some wiggle room."

"You're so cute when you're plotting things out," she said with a giggle. "Please, continue."

"We've got the feed drum in the empty stall that will hold about forty gallons," I went on. "We've got five water buckets in the trailer for horse shows, so that's twenty-five, and I think we've got five more water buckets in the barn that aren't in use, so make that fifty. That's ninety gallons I can draw up, which would keep everyone alive a second day."

Erica nodded. "That's about all I've ever been able to come up with. After that, it's hauling water in, and that's hard to do on that level."

"I'm not even sure how you would do that," I said. This was the point when I started realizing that I was playing a whole new game.

"We took the water buckets to the clinic, filled them up, and taped cardboard over the top to try and minimize the spillage on the ride back. You have to make a lot of trips."

"Let's hope it doesn't come to that," I said with a shudder.

My next problem was the fridge, freezer, and deep freeze. When it was just Angus and me, the fridge and freezer were usually empty, or close to it, so there wasn't any concern there. Here, it was a totally different situation. I pulled a few empty milk jugs out of the recycling bin and filled them with water, and put them in the deep freeze. Once they were frozen solid, they would help keep the temperature down in there.

We knew that we were going to be catching the east side of the storm, which is where the winds are the strongest, so I had to get everything inside that was in danger of blowing away or getting broken. As it turned out, that was a surprising lot of stuff. It was possible that the barn aisle could turn into a wind tunnel, so all the halters, saddle pads, tack, the cleaning supplies rack, the trash can, the stereo, and the chairs all had to go in the tack room. Then I collected the wind chimes, bird feeders, the various lawn ornaments, the potted plants, and the tomato plant towers.

Our front porch is home to a variety of things, like a shoe rack, work boots, water boots, the rocking chairs and a small table. I decided the rocking chairs were probably okay, but the rest of it needed to come in. I went around and locked all of the pasture gates so they wouldn't be flapping in the wind. I hooked the big gooseneck horse trailer up to the F-250 to stabilize it, and chocked all the wheels. I hooked up the bumper-pull trailer to my pickup, and pulled it out away from any trees that might fall on it. Erica could park the vet truck in the barn aisle to keep it safe.

Once I felt like things at the house were ready, I went to the clinic. We've had water up inside the storage shed before, and I put pallets in there after that happened. It sits in a bit of a low spot, and when it rains really hard, the water can't run off fast enough. I went in the shed and got everything up off the floor. Inside the clinic, I decided we should get everything off the floor as well, just to be on the safe side. I gathered the crew and made a plan.

"We really couldn't get more than a few inches of water in here at the very most," I reasoned. "So, if we get the computers up off the floor, and get the stuff off the bottom shelves in the pharmacy, I think we'll be okay, no matter what happens."

That went pretty fast with four people pitching in. I went back outside and gathered all the water buckets from the paddocks, the muck bucket and wheelbarrow, the bird feeder, and the hanging plants. I was amazed at how much we had sitting outside, both at home and at the clinic, that I never thought about until I had to pick it all up.

When we had done everything we could think of, I sent everyone home to get their own homes ready. We were probably going to see an emergency or two before the storm was over, but there was no reason to keep the clinic open. I went back home to check my work. The storm wasn't due to hit for another few hours, but since this was my first time trying to cover all these bases, I was really concerned about missing something important.

Lacking a generator, I decided to prepare all of the portable power options we had. I charged up the batteries for the cordless drills. Both of the drills also came with a lamp that runs off the same battery. I also charged the mobile power supply, which is basically a car battery and an inverter, all together in one. We usually use it at horse shows, and keep a solar panel plugged into it, but it will charge off a regular outlet, too.

While they were charging, we decided to bring the

donkeys and Stitches in the barn. The donkeys would have to share a stall, but that would probably make them feel better about being inside, anyway. Erica and I walked out to the back pasture together, and as we approached the riding arena, she pointed out what I had forgotten.

"The jumps have to come down," she said.

"Crapola! I knew I was forgetting something."

We dropped the halters and ran around the arena, pushing the jumps over. The last thing we wanted was a bunch of two-by-six missiles flying around. I've seen the videos of a board going right through a concrete-block wall in a storm, and leaving the jumps up would just be inviting trouble. Once they were all on the ground, we returned to our mission to get Stitches and the donkeys inside.

I was able to lure Hannah in with the food bucket and get a halter on her, but Pet was having none of it. Hannah has spent a lot of her life in a halter, so she doesn't mind it. Pet, on the other hand, only wears a halter when she's getting shots or a hoof trim or something equally hateful, so she'll run if you walk into the pasture with a halter.

Erica caught Stitches and led her over to the gate. I followed with Hannah, intending to come back and try to corner Pet. To my surprise, Pet came racing over as we were walking out the gate. I decided to keep going, and she followed along right behind Hannah. This approach had not even occurred to me as a possibility, but it ended up working like a champ. Pet followed Hannah right into the stall, and I slipped out and locked the door. There was alfalfa and water in the stall, so they consoled themselves with food, and made the best of the situation.

I felt like I was as ready as I could be. The biggest threat that we really faced was falling trees and tree limbs. Of the three quarters of a mile of dirt road between our house and the paved road, all but about one hundred yards was flanked with trees, and the power line followed the road. There were a lot of water oaks, which are known for putting down very shallow roots while growing very high, and then falling over in a strong wind. There were also a lot of pine trees, and they shed branches like they were going out of style. Between the water oaks and the pines, I felt like we had at least a fifty percent chance of our power line coming down.

Flooding wasn't much of a worry at the house, and only a minor concern at the clinic. At home, we have an active sinkhole in the woods beside the house, and it's about a twenty-foot decline to the base of it. The sinkhole drains into a cave system, so it's fairly unlikely that water would back up all the way to the barn. Both of the buildings are made out of concrete block, so I wasn't too concerned about structural damage, either, except for the roof.

Getting the cats and dogs inside was the last order of business, and with the wind picking up and thunder and lightning approaching, it wasn't too hard to get them gathered up. The rain began as we were eating supper. It started out light, and twenty minutes later, it was done.

"That was the first band," Erica announced, looking at the radar on the computer. "The next one is going to be a lot worse."

We didn't have to wait long. The wind preceded the rain this time, whipping the trees around and whistling through the barn. When the rain began, I was amazed that it was coming in completely sideways. It was actually raining in the cat door, which is impressive, because the front porch is covered by the roof, and it's twelve feet deep. I was already feeling like my prep work was not a wasted effort. I put the cover on the cat door.

The rain and wind continued to come and go as each of the bands came across us. I was exhausted from such a busy day, so I took a shower and went to bed. I knew Erica would be up most of the night, and there was no reason for both of us to lose sleep. I slept like a rock.

When I got up the next morning, the power was out. Unperturbed, I plugged the coffee pot into the inverter. I was ready, and I was going to have my coffee! Patting myself on the back for planning ahead, I added coffee and water, and pressed the 'brew' button. Nothing happened. I pressed it again. Nothing happened. I examined the screen on the inverter. When I pressed the button, the output watts spiked for a second, then fell back to zero. I realized that the coffee pot pulled too many amps for the inverter to handle. Shit!

My calm confidence shattered into a moment of near-hysteria. What was I supposed to do without coffee? This was inconceivable! I raced into the bedroom closet with my flashlight. I dug around until I found my travel toiletries bag and rooted around in it. There, among the Advil, toothpaste, shaving cream, chapstick, and travel shampoo, I found the life-saving bottle: caffeine pills.

I went back to the kitchen and washed a pill down with some water from the pitcher on the counter. I was miffed about not having my coffee, but at least I wouldn't have to deal with a withdrawal headache. As soon as it was light enough to see, I headed outside to assess the damage.

The rain was still coming and going, but the wind seemed to be done. We had little branches scattered everywhere. I walked out to the back pastures where the donkeys usually stayed. There were two large branches down, and a bunch of smaller ones, but the fence seemed to be intact.

Back in the barn, I fed everyone, and then went out front to check the rest of the pastures. There were branches down in both the front pastures. One of the pine trees had lost five big branches. The pile on the ground looked to be larger than what was still on the tree. All the fences seemed to be untouched, so I felt fairly safe about putting the horses out later.

Erica was in the barn when I came back.

"Hey, you already fed," she said.

"I figured you were up all night," I said. "I didn't want to wake you up."

"Yeah, I didn't sleep great," she admitted. "Maybe a few hours."

"I was just about to walk down the driveway and take a look at things," I said. "You want to go?"

"Sure, let me put my boots on," she said.

We walked out the gate and down the driveway. Our portion of the driveway was mostly clear. I tossed a few branches over the fence here and there. About halfway out to the pavement, we found the first major damage. A tree had fallen, taking the power lines down to the ground. Fortunately, it fell away from the road, and not across it. We kept walking.

Up near the pavement, there was a tree laying all the way across the road, blocking it from one fence to the other. The power lines were wrapped up in the branches, and I realized that they were broken free from the main power line out at the paved road. This wasn't going to be a quick fix.

As we turned around to walk back to the house, one of the neighbors drove up.

"Hey Randy, is everything alright at your house?" I asked.

"Oh yeah, we're okay. How'd you all do last night?" he asked.

"Not too bad," I said. "We've got a few branches down, but nothing serious. The main damage seems to be here and the other spot where the power lines are down."

"Same at my place," he said. "I've got the chainsaw in the back; I was just going to cut this up and get it out of the road."

"I'll give you a hand," I said. "You cut, and I'll drag it off to the side."

"Deal," he said.

The three of us managed to get the road passable in about twenty minutes. Randy gave us a ride back to our house.

"Let me know if you all need anything," he said.

"Thanks, and the same for you," I said.

One thing happened that I hadn't anticipated as being advantageous, but ended up helping us out, and that was the rain. The automatic water buckets in the pastures don't fill up all the way to the top; they usually stop about four inches down. The rain had filled them all the way to the brim, so each bucket had about ten extra gallons of water in it. That was a great help, because the power didn't come back on for three days.

On the second day, I borrowed a generator from a friend and ran the fridge and the freezer. The milk jug ice blocks helped, but two days is a long time when it's eighty-five degrees.

I rationed the water out as miserly as I could. We got rain intermittently for the first two days after the storm passed, and that helped with the field buckets. On the third day, I knew we were going to run out of water by the end of the day. Power was on at the clinic, so I loaded up all the empty buckets in the back of my truck and headed down there.

Halfway down the driveway I had to stop. There were power company trucks blocking the road, bucket trucks up in the air, and people with yellow hard hats all over the ground cutting up branches and pulling wire. I walked over to them.

"Man, am I glad to see you guys!" I said. "This is like Christmas!"

I got a few chuckles, but I could tell they were tired. "I want you guys to know we appreciate what you've been doing the last few days. I'm sure there are plenty of people giving you grief about having to wait, but you won't get anything like that from us."

"I appreciate you saying that," said one of the guys. "We're going as fast as we can. We'll have you done in about an hour."

I backed up the driveway and unloaded the empty buckets back at the barn. Sure enough, the power was back on in an hour. I wandered around in a daze, looking at all the stuff that needed to go back to its normal place, and all the tree branches to be picked up. It was a mess, but it was also a success. We made it through, and learned some lessons.

Two weeks later we bought a generator that was capable of running the whole house, and had it installed. The power will probably never go out again, now that we're prepared, but if it does, we'll have coffee, water, refrigerator, and lights!

14

Horse Show Madness

Erica loves horse shows. My enthusiasm is waning slightly, as the novelty has worn off, but all I have to do to feel better about going to a horse show is remember every job I have ever had, and consider that I could be doing that right now, rather than this. It's all about perspective.

On this particular week in November, the horse show in question was in Venice, Florida, which is on the Gulf coast just south of Sarasota. It's not the closest horse show, but South Florida is a pretty decent place to be in the wintertime, with lows in the fifties and highs in the eighties. There are worse places to be.

It takes a bit of getting ready to go to a horse show. Not only do I have to get everything ready to go that we're taking with us, but I also have to make sure everything that is staying is ready for the farm sitter. Mostly what that consists of is making sure that there is enough feed for all the horses, dogs and cats, and that there are clear instructions on everyone's feed and medication regime.

We were planning to leave on Wednesday morning, so I spent most of Tuesday getting ready. First off, I went to the feed store and loaded up on critter groceries. I do this every Tuesday, so that part wasn't unusual. I stopped by the gas station and filled up the truck with diesel. That part is important, because if I forget to do that (and I have), then I will either have to stop at a truck stop on the way south, or unhook the trailer and go fill up, delaying our departure. The problem is that there is not a gas station that sells diesel in our area that has a big enough parking lot for me to get the big horse trailer into. They just weren't designed for trailers.

When I got home, I unloaded feed into the feed room at the front of the barn, and then hooked up the trailer. We have a twenty-eight foot gooseneck trailer, with a tack room in the front end. The back end is called a center load design, which means the ramp is in the middle of one side, and you have two stalls in the front, and two stalls in the back. The back end also opens up as a ramp. This is helpful if you have a horse that is not excited about getting in the trailer, as you can open the back and the side, and then they can see through. It's much less scary that way. You have to remember that most horses assume that they are going to be eaten by a lion at any given moment. It's a prey animal thing; you wouldn't understand.

I pulled the trailer around by the barn for easy access. Since we had a three and a half hour drive down Interstate 75, I decided to check the tire pressure on the truck and trailer. This is a time-consuming chore, because once I start airing up tires, my OCD kicks in, and I have to get them exactly the same pressure. The truck tires have to be seventy psi, and the trailer tires have to be one hundred psi. While I was in maintenance mode, I went ahead and checked all the fluids on the truck. I was glad that I did all that, because there was one low tire on the truck, and we were low on coolant. The last thing I want is to be changing a tire on the side of the interstate. Just in case, though, I took my cordless impact wrench and put it in the back seat. Chance favors a prepared mind. A quick wash of the windows and mirrors, and I felt like the truck and trailer were roadworthy.

Next came the part that I was dreading: lugging two bales of hay into the trailer. There is no easy way to carry the hay, and lifting one hundred and twenty pounds by the strings that hold it together is really hard on the hands. I have tried hay hooks, which work great on compressed bales, but they tear right out of these. I wrestled a bale into the wheelbarrow, which is actually a four-wheel dump cart, and dragged it out to the trailer. I was feeling brave, so I tried to pull it up the ramp. Because the hay bale is longer than the cart, it sticks over the back end, which means the weight is centered over the rear axle. As soon as I got the back wheels on the ramp, it flipped over backwards. I really should have known better.

I carried the hay bale into the trailer and side-scrabbled it to the front of a stall. This is the hard part, because there is just not quite enough room to actually carry the bale into the stall, either sideways or straight on. I felt like the people who determined the dimensions for these bales didn't ever carry them into trailers like this. I righted the cart and brought the second bale out, and because I am a fast learner, I didn't bother trying to pull it up the ramp again.

The feed came next. In case you don't know, horse feed comes in fifty-pound sacks. This is a fairly functional system, but the sacks don't travel well once they are opened. My work-around, so that I don't have to mess with that, is buckets. We have four buckets that originally had some sort of feed supplement in them. They are square, they have flip-up lids that are attached so they can't be lost, and they hold about three gallons, so they don't weigh a ton even when they're full of horse pellets. I scoop the exact amount of feed I need for each horse (plus one meal, just in case) into these buckets, snap the lid down, and stack them neatly beside the hay in the trailer. Perfect!

I'm what other people sometimes refer to as an over-preparer. I make a list of all the things that might happen, and then try to figure out what I would need to deal with those situations. That's why I take the cordless impact wrench, as it speeds up the tire-changing process considerably. It's also why I take extra feed and a bucket or two of emergency water for the horses. If the truck breaks down, the horses could be stuck in the trailer for hours. If it happens while we're at the horse show, they might end up staying there an extra day. I've seen it happen to other people. So, in the spirit of being prepared, I filled up the emergency water and loaded it with the feed.

I left the tack and medicine for Erica to pack. Both of those are filled with ever-changing variables, and I just don't even bother trying to keep up with it. How hard could it be, you ask? They need a saddle, saddle pad, girth, and a bridle. I laugh, because I was once so naïve. The problem is that in our tack room, there is a wall with a hook rack running the entire length of it. Every hook has as many bridles as it can hold, or some other leather thing that I don't know the name of. There are standing martingales, running martingales, draw reins, straps to go around the chest, straps that go around the neck, various variations of all these things and more in different styles, or lengths, and what we used last week might not be what we use this week. So: I leave it alone.

We use the trailer pretty regularly, so the stalls always have bedding in them. I added a little more, just so that there was plenty of absorbent stuff for the horses to stand on. This makes cleaning the trailer a little easier. If you don't have horses, you might not know that horse trailers are a natural laxative for them. As soon as they get in, they poop. Vespa will also pee within ten seconds of getting on the trailer, every time, but Ernie usually tries to hold it. If you are driving more than thirty minutes, they will probably poop again. It's just how it is. Lastly, I loaded up two hay nets with alfalfa for Ernie and Vespa to munch on during the ride south and hung them in their trailer stalls.

With the exception of packing a suitcase, my horse show prep was done. I went upstairs to do the laundry and make a pile of groceries to take with us. I have to eat pretty regularly, or else I get hangry, which is a combination of hungry and angry. Erica doesn't suffer from this at all, which I am envious of, but she has recognized that I have it in spades, so we always have boxes of protein and granola bars, crackers, and sandwich stuff when we go to a horse show, or any other such place. We also take a five-gallon water cooler, because staying hydrated on the road can get expensive without it.

On Wednesday, we loaded the last of the personal items, the horses, and some road trip snacks, and off we went. Being a veterinarian, Erica is incapable of not doing something work-related on the way, so we stopped at a lab in Ocala and dropped off some blood that needed to be tested. Once that was done, we got on the interstate and started laying down miles.

We use this time to listen to a variety of podcasts. Usually they are either about business or personal development, and often result in a brainstorming session. A lot of our business practices and growth and development practices have come from these road trips. It's a great time for both of us to focus on these things and discuss the veterinary clinic, as the outside distractions are limited in the truck. It's also the only time I ever get Erica for three hours of [mostly] uninterrupted time.

I have to say that podcasts are a technological bonus that I never expected, but which have turned out to be a wonderful asset. There are podcasts on just about any topic of interest you can imagine. I love human-interest podcasts like This American Life and Radio Lab, science and space exploration shows, psychology and self-improvement shows, writing and publishing podcasts, all kinds of stuff. There is literally something for everyone. I have learned so much from them about things that I care about, and it's all free! If you haven't discovered podcasts yet, you're missing out.

As is usually the case, Tammy, who is Erica's trainer, was already at the horse show, and was ready for Erica to ride the instant we arrived. We did what I call the "Rapid Unload

Sequence A" in which we stack all the stuff in front of a stall and organize it later. I generally get things set up while she's riding in the warm up ring, so it works out okay.

If you've never been to a horse show, then there are a few things you need to know about horse shows. First off, "horse show" is a generic term that applies to about six hundred different things. To be more accurate, I should say that it applies to about six hundred different disciplines. A barrel race is a horse show, as is a hunter/jumper competition, a Dressage show, western reining, a cart and buggy driving course, an Arab halter class, and a mule and donkey extravaganza, just to name a few. Basically, it's any competition of any kind involving horses, except for jousting, which falls under the umbrella of "things that people should not do."

Erica is involved in the Hunter/Jumper world. This is an English riding discipline, and consists of a series of jumps, or fences, set up in a complex course. The height of the fence rails depends on what class it is, anywhere from about two feet up to about six feet, and there are several different variations of competition. The purpose of them all is for the horse and rider to negotiate the course as fast as possible and jump all the fences without knocking any of the rails down.

To make the courses exciting, they change the layout after every class. This means the rider has to memorize the course in a few minutes, and then get the horse through it. This is complicated by the decorations. The jumps themselves are very much works of art, and you never know what kind of bizarre and interesting jumps you will see. There are also potted plants, flowers, and small trees everywhere. This makes the courses very appealing to people looking at it, and very sinister to horses running around it. The horses tend to spook at all of these sorts of things, so part of the discipline is the relationship of trust and control that you have with your horse.

At a horse show like this one, which starts on Thursday and goes through Sunday, you ride your horse in one or two classes each day. If you have two or three horses that you are riding, then you ride each of them in a class each day. Depending on the course, it usually takes somewhere around a minute to ride a course. The rest of the time is generally spent washing and primping the horse, cleaning tack and gear, cleaning stalls, catching up with friends you haven't seen since the last horse show, and so on. Here in Venice, we try to make it to the beach a few times, too.

Most everyone has a trainer, who is teaching them how to jump better, and improving horsemanship, and so on, and most trainers have more than one student at the horse show. The trainer is the center of scheduling and arranging things. Erica's trainer had four students at this particular show. We are all in the same barn, and even though there isn't a team thing in the competition part of things, there is very much a sense of camaraderie and team among everyone. It's pretty cool to be a part of that kind of thing. The majority of people in this particular sport are teenage girls, but Erica's team is three adult women and one teenage girl. That makes the bonding part a little easier for a forty-year-old guy like me. We all go watch each other ride, and cheer everyone on. When someone falls off their horse on the course, which happens sometimes, everyone else is there to help, and that is an invaluable thing.

On the second day at Venice, the actual show jumping got started. Erica spent the morning washing horses and getting ready. There really wasn't much that I could do to help at this point, so I settled into my chair with a book. A great deal of horse showing is ritual washing, as I have learned. I used to try to help wash, until I realized that it isn't about getting the horse clean, it's about getting your game face on. So much of this sport is psychology; the preparations are about getting your head screwed on straight and giving your hands something to do while you're working on that.

"Okay, you want to help me get saddled up?" Erica asked, poking her head around the corner. Ernie poked his wet head around the corner too, but seemed disappointed that I didn't have a carrot for him. My whole job during the horse show is to give Ernie and Vespa a carrot after they come out of the ring. I think that has created some sort of expectation with Ernie.

"Sure," I said. "Just let me finish this book. I only have like two hundred pages to go."

"Very funny," she said, leading Ernie into his stall.

I got up and stretched, and went to the tack stall to get the saddle and tack. Erica was combing out Ernie's tail when I brought everything in. She sat the brush down and saddled him up, giving his tail a few more swipes when she was done. I put his hackamore on and led him out of the stall to the mounting block. Erica put on her helmet, adjusted Ernie's gear a bit, and hopped on.

"Go fast," I smiled, patting her on the leg. "And Ernie, make sure she stays on, no matter what. Your carrot is dependent on that." Ernie looked the other way and pretended not to hear my idle threats.

I grabbed a few carrots and made my way to the ring. Hunter/Jumper shows are not a spectator sport, and in all but the very biggest money classes, there is no place to sit and watch. Trainers stand by the ring gate, and team members just stand by the fence.

After warming up in the practice ring, it was their turn. I always video each course so that Erica can see what she did right, and what she could have done better. If she falls off the horse and gets hurt, I also have video support for my argument that she should find something safer to do, like knitting. I readied my camera as they entered the ring. They started off really strong, with Erica choosing a good line from the first jump to the second. This is important, because if she goes too wide, or cuts it too tight, Ernie will be off by half a stride, which means he will either be too far away to make the jump, in which case he will probably slam on the brakes and refuse the jump, or they will be too close, and he will knock the fence down as he tries to jump it.

They cleared the second fence perfect, and made a sweeping turn around the back side of the ring to the third fence. This one was a two-jump design called an In and Out. It's two fences set one stride apart, so you have to jump the first fence at just the right speed to land in the right place to launch over the second fence. Something went wrong, but I was too far away to tell what. All I knew for sure was that the rail came down on the first fence of the third jump.

They cleared the rest of the course perfectly and well within the allotted time, but because they had a rail down, they didn't qualify for the jump-off. The jump-off is a tie-breaker for those who make it around the course with no time faults and no rails down, and whoever has the fastest time in the jump-off and the least amount of rails down wins. I met them just outside the ring to perform my sacred duty, as Erica and her trainer talked about the ride.

"That was a great ride,"Tammy said. "You were perfect on your line to every single jump except on number three."

I broke a carrot in half and fed it to Ernie, patting him on the neck.

"I couldn't see the distance when I came around the corner from two," Erica said. "It just wouldn't happen, and then we were on top of it by the time I could tell we were off."

"If you can't see the distance, you've got to look away for a minute,"Tammy said. "You got locked down, and if you don't see a distance, you aren't ever going to see it unless you look away and reset your perspective. But still, you did really good! You were calm, and Ernie was calm, and overall it was a really solid ride."

Ernie had consumed both carrots and caught his breath by the time they got done with the post-ride coaching session, and we walked back to the barn.

"I'm going to give Ernie a bath," Erica said. "Would you mind picking his stall and checking out his water buckets?"

"You mean his tea buckets," I corrected. Ernie has this thing about shoving hay into his water buckets, which he does every single day. It probably makes the water taste good, but it makes for a bit of work scrubbing the dried hay bits and stuff off the inside of the bucket. "No problem, I've got it under control."

"Thanks," she replied. "I can do it after I wash him if you'd rather go read."

I think Erica feels guilty sometimes about horse shows, mainly because the only major thrill and excitement at a horse show is the one minute of actually jumping fences, and I don't do that. I appreciate that she recognizes that. I honestly don't mind it though, because as I said earlier, it's way better than any other job I've ever had, and besides, we're a team. I know she doesn't enjoy everything about writer's conferences, but she still goes with me. That's just what we do.

"Nope, I've got it," I assured her. "I'll be done with that and back to reading my book before you get the shampoo on him, anyway."

"Alright," she agreed. "Once I get tack cleaned, do you want to go walk on the beach?"

"Absolutely!"

I have a thing about the ocean, some sort of connection that I don't really understand. Really, it's more of a connection to water; it doesn't necessarily have to be the ocean, but the more often I go spend time in or near water, the better I feel, emotionally. It has a calming effect on me. Maybe it's a negative ion environment, or maybe I was a fish or something in a past life, I don't know. What I do know is that I never pass on an opportunity to go get wet!

I'm not one of those people who likes to go lay in the hot sun and fry next to thousands of other people frying in the hot sun on a beach. If we go in the summer time, it's usually at either sunrise, or sunset. The temperature is much more reasonable, it's much less crowded, and you can really get plugged into nature instead of dodging kids, Frisbees, and footballs.

Since it was a Thursday afternoon in the middle of November, there weren't very many people at the beach. The temperature was in the high seventies, and there was a light breeze blowing. Yes, as you are probably recognizing, it was absolutely amazing! We took off our socks and shoes and left them on the end of the boardwalk that leads from the parking lot across the sand dunes to the beach.

I find the wildlife at the beach to be absolutely fascinating. My very favorite things to watch are pelicans. They get in a line, sometimes two or three, and sometimes eight or ten, and skim the surface of the water. I don't know what kind of speeds they achieve, but their wing tips are only an inch from the water as they sail by, rarely flapping; just cruising effortlessly. I'm mesmerized as they go by, knowing that just a little peak of a wave could catch a wing and bring them crashing down, but it never happens.

The shore birds are also great fun to watch. They race up and down the beach at the edge of the water, pecking little bites of food out of the sand. As the surf recedes between waves, they race out and try to find something to eat in the momentarily-exposed sea floor, and then race back ahead of the next wave to avoid being drenched. They almost never take flight to avoid the waves; they just run at seemingly impossible speeds for such little birds.

One of the interesting features of the beaches at Venice is the sand itself. If you dumped out a pepper shaker, and then poured the salt shaker on top of it and mixed them together, that would be about the color of the sand there. It's much darker than any other beach I've seen. There is also an interesting shell deposit along the surf line. There's a strip about three feet wide of sea shells that's right along the high tide line. Most of the shells are pulverized, and in various stages of becoming sand, but some of the smaller shells are intact. I scanned it closely as we walked slowly down the beach.

"Oh, look at that one," Erica said, reaching down and pulling up a shell fragment. "It's got a purple hue on the inside." She held it up to the sun, and we could see the outer colors contrasting with the inner colors.

"That's pretty good," I agreed.

A little further down the beach, a large piece of rose-col-ored shell caught my eye. It was in the water line, and was gone before I could grab it. I stood for a moment, waiting to see if it would reappear. The water was clear, and I watched in fascination as the incoming waves spread the shells out, then picked them up in a swirl as they receded. It was a real-time example of the shells being continuously smashed against each other, mixed around, dispersed, and smashed again, over and over in the process of natural recycling.

"Check this one out," I said, snatching a tiny, bleached-white fragment from the water. We looked at it closely, trying to make out the minute details. It was a cylinder, about the same diameter as a coffee stirrer. It was about an inch long, and had tiny, yet intricate polyps all over it. "I think this is a piece of coral."

"I think so, too," she said. "Look at how the lines and patterns are on those little things. They look like tiny flowers!"

We found a few more interesting shells, but no shark teeth, which this area is famous for. At last, the moment arrived that I like the most, which is sunset. There were a few wispy clouds in the western sky, and as the sun neared the horizon, these turned orange, then pink, deepening towards red. There was a moment when the sun seemed to drip down, and the water reached up to meet it. Erica grabbed my hand, and we watched in silence.

A small group of pelicans flew across the horizon, sil-houetted black against the sun for a moment as they passed. The gentles waves lapped the shore, providing a steady rhythm for the cries of the shore birds to play against. Now that the sun had touched the horizon, it seemed to speed up in its descent. I could see it continuously drop now, as it reached the halfway point, and after that it shrank rapidly. The perfection of the moment was accentuated by the swiftness of its passing. A moment later, it was gone, leaving only the painted clouds to show that it was ever there.

The rest of the weekend went largely the same. Erica won two of her classes, which earned her two blue ribbons to hang with the others on her trainer's banner. This is a horse show tradition. Each trainer has a banner that they hang on their tack stall, and all their students hang their ribbons on the trainer's banner. By the end of the horse show, you generally can't see the banner anymore. It's a team pride thing.

On Sunday afternoon, it was time to pack up and head home. This is always tough. For Erica, it marks the end of the fun, and a return to the real world. For me, it means three or four hours of fighting traffic on a crowded highway with the trailer, and fragile cargo. In some ways, it's also a relief, because it means I can get back to my regular exercise routine, and get away from the restaurant food and back to home cooking, and of course, back to our fabulous bed. There are some things that just can't be replicated on the road.

15

Sleepless Nights

I stretched out in bed, exhausted from the day. I considered reading for a few minutes to help my brain unwind, but considering such things with one's eyes closed generally doesn't work out, and this time was no exception. I didn't even realize that I had dozed off until Erica's phone rang. Her current ringtone is *Staying Alive* by the Bee Gees, and I can assure you that it will bring you out of a dead sleep. I looked at the alarm clock as she answered: 10:32 pm. I had only been asleep for about twenty minutes.

"Hello, Dr. Lacher."

I listened to her side of the conversation, trying to determine if I could go back to sleep or not.

"Okay, if he wants to lie down, I'm okay with that, as long as he isn't flailing," she said with a chuckle. Her calm demeanor and faint humor almost always soothed the stressed-out horse owner on the other end of the phone, and it also told me we were about to go to work. "Just let him lay quietly, and we'll be there as fast as we can."

I groaned as I sat up. "Where's this one at?" I asked.

"High Springs, on the other side," she said. "Mary Denmore's new gelding, I think his name is Flash Gordon."

"Well, at least it isn't an hour away." Dressing as quick as I could, I glanced longingly at the bed one last time. "Goodbye pillow, I miss you already!"

Out in the kitchen, a line of eager assistants waited at the door. Both dogs, of course, and three of the five cats. They didn't actually want to go with us, they just wanted to go outside and prowl around in the dark. We did the weaving dance of squirming out the door while keeping them all inside with a foot and a hand.

I drove, as I always do. Erica sat in the passenger seat, laptop open. She always looks over the patient history to make sure she's up to speed with the animal's health. Despite being deprived of my anticipated bedtime, I always get a rush of excitement when we have an emergency. You never know what's waiting for you. I turned up the radio as we bounced down our long driveway. It's almost a mile to the asphalt from our house, which is generally a good thing, but when you're in a rush, it seems like it takes forever.

Twenty-five minutes later, we pulled into their driveway. Erica gave me the gate code, which I entered on the keypad. As the gate opened, I looked around. The barn lights were on, but I could also see a flashlight bobbing around in the field off to the left of the barn. We eased up the driveway to the barn.

"Go to the left," Erica pointed. "I think there's a gate in the fence over there by that tree."

I switched the headlights to bright as we pulled around the barn. We bounced up and down as we crept across the field, and I finally spotted the gate. There was someone standing by it, probably one of Mary's kids. He opened the gate as we approached, and I rolled down the window.

"Just head towards mom over there," he pointed. "It's safe, there ain't nothing to run over out there."

"Okie dokie," I replied. We finally neared the flashlight, and I switched the headlights back to dim as the downed horse came into view.

"Stay back a bit so we can keep the headlights pointed that way," Erica directed. "Don't point them right at him, but just off to the side so we can see."

I parked, and we hopped out, leaving the engine running. As soon as I got out of the driver's seat, a black lab appeared out of the darkness and hopped into it, surprising the hell out of me.

"Booger, get outa there!" Mary whistled, nearly shattering my eardrum. Booger hopped back out onto the ground, immediately disappearing into the darkness.

Erica went over to the horse, talking to Mary. I grabbed the flashlight out of the door pocket and went around back and opened the lift gate. Booger appeared again, sniffing everything, his tail swatting my legs. I gave his ears a quick scratch.

"Hey buddy-buddy," I whispered. "Give me just a minute, and I'll give you a good fuss."

I quickly grabbed the tray out of the top left drawer of the vet box, which is a huge box that fills the whole back end of the SUV. It has lots of drawers, and holds most everything a veterinarian needs, except for really big items. I pulled out the head lamp, the stethoscope, the lactate meter, a syringe to draw blood for the lactate meter, the thermometer, a sleeve (which is a disposable glove that goes all the way up to your armpit), and a bottle of lubricant.

"Okay, we're going to try to get him up," Erica said as I walked over. "He's been down for a while, so he may have trouble if his legs have gone to sleep."

I sat the tray down on the hood to keep Booger out of it and went over and took the lead rope from Mary. Erica got behind the horse and grabbed his tail.

"Okay Flash, let's get up," she said, giving me the nod. I tugged on the lead rope as Erica lifted his tail. All this really does is irritate a horse, mind you. You'll never lift one up by hand. Flash shook his head, and I gave him plenty of slack as he extended his front legs. He didn't quite make it up on the first try, and didn't seem interested in a second effort.

"Hey buddy-buddy," I said softly, trying to keep him calm. "Let's go, you don't want her to get the pliers out."

It was too late; Erica was already opening her Leatherman. A slight pinch with the pliers on the sensitive area at the base of his tail was enough to give Flash a change of heart. With renewed enthusiasm, he reared back, and with a mighty shove on the rear legs, he made it to his feet.

"Yay, that's a good boy!" I cheered for him, patting his neck. "We're going to get you all fixed up, don't you worry about it."

Erica grabbed the tray off the truck and began her exam.

She listened to his heart, then his breathing, and then moved back to his abdomen and listened to his gut sounds. Satisfied with what she heard, she came up and lifted his lip, checking the color of his gums.

"Okay," she said to Mary, "his heart rate is low, which is good, and his breathing is pretty normal, considering how hard he worked to get up just now. I can hear some gut sounds, so that's a good sign too. I'm going to give him some drugs, and then palpate him and we'll see if we can tell what's going on."

"So, you don't think he's twisted his guts up?" she asked. "I've been afraid to let him lay down, because I didn't want him to get twisted up."

"Oh no, he definitely hasn't twisted anything," Erica replied. "If he was twisted, he would be throwing himself all over the place, screaming, flailing, and you wouldn't have any doubt about what was happening."

Mary relaxed visibly. She was short and round, and had one of those faces that doesn't hide a thing, framed by short, dark, curly hair.

"And just so you know," Erica continued, "that's not how that works. When a colic turns into a twist, the twist happens while they're standing. It has to do with gas, distension, and internal spasms. When they start rolling and flailing, they're in serious pain from that, and they're trying to make it stop hurting. So, the twist isn't caused by rolling; rolling is a result of a twist."

"I didn't know that," said Mary. "I always heard the rolling caused it."

"Nope," Erica grinned, "that's just an old wives' tale." She disappeared around the back of the truck to pull some drugs. I stood there holding Flash, and scratching Booger, who had reappeared.

"Don't feel bad," I said. "Most people are under that same impression. And hey, it makes sense, right? Horse rolls over, guts get twisted. Until it's your horse rolling around, it's not something you think too much about, anyway."

"Sure," said Mary. "It sounds reasonable, so I never questioned it." I could tell she was relieved. Erica has that affect on most people, which is one of her superpowers. "This is the first colic I've ever had. I've had three different horses over the last twenty years, and none of them ever got sick. I guess I panicked a little." She grinned. "I'm so glad you guys came out here. I really had no idea what to do."

"Hey, this is what we do," I said with a laugh. "That's why you have a vet."

Erica came back around into the light, pulled some blood, and then gave Flash two shots in the vein in his neck. I pulled the lactate meter out of its case and stuck a test strip in the top. It looks just like a blood tester that diabetics use, and functions in basically the same way, only it tests for different things in the blood. Erica put a drop of blood on the strip, and we waited.

"Two point three," she announced. "That's great, that means he's going to be fine. Anything under three is good. Colics that have a serious problem like a twist, or a section of intestine that's lost blood supply, those guys will have a lactate of five or six, and that means they need surgery immediately. Flash doesn't have any of those symptoms, so he's probably just got an impaction, and a little gas built up. I'm going to palpate him, and we'll see what we've got."

She pulled on the sleeve and applied a liberal amount of lube. I held the lead rope and stepped to the side that Erica was on so I could see everything. Even though Flash was sedated now, he was still fully capable of kicking, rearing, or taking off. None of these things happen very often (and never to me personally, or at least not yet), but when your wife has her arm buried to the shoulder inside the rectum of a twelve-hundred-pound horse who doesn't feel good, you don't take any chances. My job here was to keep the horse's head turned slightly towards Erica. This forces him to put his weight on the rear leg closest to her, which will make it so that he can't kick her. She felt around inside him for a moment, then pulled her arm back out and came up and took the lead rope from me.

"Okay, everything is where it's supposed to be," she announced. "He's got a decent impaction, and he's a little bit dehydrated. The drugs I gave him will help him relax on the inside, and we're going to over-hydrate him, which will help push everything through."

I took my cue and went to the back of the truck to get the bucket, tube, salt mix, and hand pump. I also grabbed the folding stool to sit on while pumping water into the horse, having done this a time or two before. I learned early on that trying to squat down and pump water for fifteen minutes will kill my knees. I filled the bucket with water from the trough at the fence and brought everything over.

The tube went up Flash's nose which he, understandably, didn't like at all. He tossed his head up and down, blowing and snorting. I did my best to hold him still, which was fairly ineffectual. All the activity got his nose bleeding a bit, which meant that every time he snorted, he covered us in a fine mist of blood. This happens sometimes, and I didn't really pay any attention to it, or at least, not until Booger realized what was happening. Booger made it his mission to lick all the blood off of us, which was admirable, but it did make the process with Flash a bit more challenging.

Mary grabbed Booger and held him in a bear hug. "Susie, for God's sake, come get Booger!" she shouted. Susie had apparently been watching everything from some secret vantage point in the darkness nearby, as I didn't even know she was there until she ran up and grabbed the dog. "We're trying to keep Flash alive here, and Booger is right in the middle of things." Booger wagged his tail.

At last, Erica gave me the nod, which meant she was in the stomach and it was time for me to get busy. I stuck the tube onto the pump, sat down on my stool, and pumped five or six times. I pulled the hose back off the pump to check for reflux, which is water on the stomach that isn't going on through. Horses are physically incapable of vomiting, even though they need to sometimes, and a lot of water siphoning back out of the tube in this situation would tell us that there is a more serious problem. Since there was no reflux, I added the salt mix to the bucket, stirred it in, and began pumping in earnest.

"So, what this does is replace electrolytes, pulls water into the gut, and dissolves the impaction," Erica explained. "The stuff in the salt mix is a lot like Gatorade without the sugar."

"So, you don't put mineral oil in them?" Mary asked.

"Nope, that's an outdated practice," Erica answered. "Mineral oil doesn't actually break down an impaction. It does lube everything up, but it mainly just makes a hell of a mess. Water will dissolve the impaction." She glanced at

Susie. "That makes a great science experiment to gross out the kids at school," she said, conspiratorially. "Take two balls of horse poop. Put one in a clear cup with water, and the other one in a cup with mineral oil. See what happens to each piece of poop over an hour or two."

Mary laughed. "Wow, I'm learning all kinds of stuff tonight," she said. "I feel so much better; not knowing what was happening was really scary."

I finished pumping the last of the water, tipping the bucket over a bit to get the salt that hadn't dissolved yet. Erica gently pulled the tube out, leaning away to the side as Flash sneezed, spraying me with blood, snot, bits of hay, and water. Booger broke free from Susie and ran over, trying to lick my arms, face, and shirt all at the same time.

"Booger!" Mary chastised him, which fell on deaf ears.

"Oh, he's alright," I laughed, scratching his back as he cleaned me up. "This way I won't have to take a shower when we get home!"

"Ewww," Susie pretended to throw up. "Booger's gross. He licks his butt all day."

"Susie!" Mary turned to her. "Seriously!"

"Well, he does," she said.

I fended the dog off long enough to stand up. I gathered up our stuff, cleaning the gear at the water trough and stowing everything as Erica typed up the care instructions and processed the payment. Once my part was done, I wrestled with Booger a bit more, scratching his chest until I found that magic spot.

"There it is, yes, I found it," I said, laughing as his back leg kicked at warp speed. "I knew you had one, I just had to find it."

Flash stood where we left him, head drooping, swaying slightly. "He ought to be feeling better pretty quick," Erica said. "If he's not interested in eating in an hour, call me. If he is interested in food, then just follow the instructions on feed portions."

"I'm gonna stay up with him all night," Susie announced.

Erica laughed. "Well, I hope that isn't necessary! As long as he's eating by midnight, you ought to be able to go to bed."

"Thank you guys so much," Mary said again. "You don't know how much I appreciate you doing this."

"Well, that's what we do," Erica said. "Make sure you call me if you have any questions, or if he isn't looking better. I don't care what time it is."

"Okay, I sure will." Mary gave Erica a big hug. This had happened so many times that it didn't even faze me anymore. People just love Erica. I get it; I think she's the most amazing woman there ever was.

We drove home with the windows down and the radio up, singing along with Elton John at the top of our lungs. By the time we got through the shower and fell into bed again, it was nearly one in the morning. The phone didn't ring again, which is always a good sign. As tired as I was, I might not have heard it anyway. Reading a bit of my book never even crossed my mind as I closed my eyes this time. The frogs singing in the woods just outside my open window put me to sleep in seconds.

16

That Sinking Sensation

Erica and I were sitting in the spare bedroom/recording studio one Saturday morning. One of the things we do to fulfill our mission, which is to make the world a better place for horses, is produce a podcast called *Straight from the Horse Doctor's Mouth*. We cover all kinds of horse-health topics to help people understand the needs of their horses more clearly, and we were about to begin recording our next episode when Erica's phone rang. I leaned back in my seat and waited as she listened.

"Wow. Yeah, that's not good."

Silence. Sometimes it's painful to only catch one side of a discussion.

"No, no, no, no, no. Don't do that. Don't do anything like that. Tell him to stop."

More silence. She turned to me and waved her finger, the hand signal that we're going to work. I shut down the recording equipment and followed her down to the driveway. Whatever it was, it was serious.

"Yeah, the problem is, the ground is probably very unstable. If he drives the backhoe over to her, they could both disappear in a cave-in. Does that make sense? We have to assume the worst. Is she panicking?"

I drove down the driveway, desperately trying to figure out what was going on. I've seen some eyebrow-raising stuff on horse emergencies, but never anything that involved a backhoe. When we got to the pavement, Erica pointed to the left.

"Okay. I'm on my way. Don't do anything until I get there." She hung up the phone and looked at me. "Bella is in a sinkhole."

"Who's Bella?"

"She's a blind horse. We removed one of her eyes five or six years ago, and the other one about two years ago."

"Well, no wonder she walked into a sinkhole," I said.

"No, it formed underneath her. The ground collapsed, and she's standing in a hole. Mike wants to try to dig her out with the backhoe."

The conversation I had listened to was starting to make a lot more sense. I was still having a hard time picturing the situation. All the sinkholes I had seen at that point in my life were deep cones, like an inside-out volcano. If a horse was at the bottom of one of those, I had no idea how we were going to get it out. Erica was right, though, a backhoe was not a good idea. Even if the ground was stable, which it obviously wasn't, Bella wouldn't be able to see what was happening, and running a backhoe close by her would probably send her into a panic. I decided to speed up a little more.

While I drove, Erica pulled up the phone number for the Technical Large Animal Emergency Rescue (TLAER) team at the University of Florida and gave them a call.

"Hi, this is Dr. Lacher with Springhill Equine Veterinary Clinic. I have a client with a blind horse trapped in a freshly formed sinkhole. I'm on my way to the scene, but I wanted to alert you that we may need your help. I'll be able to give you more information in about fifteen minutes."

She answered a few questions, and they hung up. I didn't even know there *was* a rescue team for large animals, but I didn't say so, as Erica was deep in thought, and I didn't want to interrupt her. We made a few more turns and headed out into the country west of Newberry.

The aquifer is very close to the surface in Florida, and it constantly erodes the soft limestone tunnels as it flows to the surface in the form of springs, which dump into rivers and run to the coast. Sinkholes are very common here, occurring when the limestone gets too thin to support the ground above it. The roof of the tunnel collapses, and the ground above drops the corresponding amount. If it's a little tunnel, it will be a little sinkhole. If it's a big tunnel or a cave, it can be a massive sinkhole, big enough to swallow a large building. Sometimes that will seal off the tunnel, and the water has to find another route. In those cases, you can fill the hole in at the surface, and that's it. Other times, the water is able to push the debris out of the way, and the hole is perpetually open after that, unable to be filled. This is called a karst window. Which one Bella was dealing with remained to be seen, but if it was the second kind, then time was of the essence, and the ground could fall out from under her at any moment.

When we arrived at their farm, Erica pointed me to a large pasture beside the house. "They're out there, somewhere. Pull on down to the end. I think there's a gate."

"I'm not real confident about driving around out there," I said. "Should we park out here on the road?"

"Let's see where they are, and what the situation looks like."

It was a large pasture, most flat, and dotted with a few trees here and there. Erica opened the gate, and I carefully pulled in. My skin was crawling at the thought of being swallowed up by the earth, even though I understood how these things work. My rational brain might know that we were unlikely to create a second sinkhole, but it was having a hard time competing with the irrational part of my brain that has read all of Stephen King's books.

At first, we couldn't see them. As I pulled up on a low rise, we spotted a bizarre spectacle. A woman was sitting on the ground about two hundred yards away, and a horse head was in front of her, nibbling at the grass at her feet. No horse in sight, just the head at ground level.

"Ho-ly shit," I muttered. "We're going to stop right here and walk over." I snapped a picture with my phone as we stepped out of the vet truck.

"Make sure you talk out loud when we get over there," Erica said. "Bella can't see you, so you have to make noise, so she knows what's going on."

"Got it."

As we walked up, I got a better view of the situation. The hole was about the same size as Bella. Her rump was touching the back, and her neck was against the front. There was a bit of space on each side, but not more than a foot or two. The flat of her back was slightly above ground level. Kelly, her owner, stood up as we drew near.

"Bella, what are you doing in that hole?" Erica called out.

"It looks like she's pretty calm," I said. "I doubt that I'd be handling it this well if it were me."

"She's been really calm," Kelly said. "I was afraid she would be panicking without Patches. They're joined at the hip most of the time, but she's just standing here eating grass."

Erica spoke softly to Bella as she walked up to the hole and got down on her hands and knees. "Easy, girl. I'm just going to check you out and see if you're hurt." She ran her hands over Bella's upper legs and shined a flashlight down into the hole. Bella continued to graze, unfazed. Erica crawled around the hole, slowing making a full circle as she checked out the horse and the hole. When she was finished, she back up from the edge a few feet and stood up.

"She seems to be fine, at least, as far as I can see from up here. Do you know how long she's been in there?"

Kelly shrugged. "I have no idea. We turned them out around eight last night, and she didn't come in with everyone else this morning. You know she stays glued to Patches, so we knew something was wrong."

Erica pointed to the edge of the hole. "She's been grazing for a while, but there's only two poops in the hole that I can see. I don't think she was in there all night." The grass on the front edge of the hole had been grazed down close in an arc as far as she could reach in every direction. "I'm going to get the Technical Large Animal Emergency Rescue team out here. We're not even going to try to get her out of there on our own."

She pulled out her phone and walked away a few steps. I looked back at Bella and tried to come up with a theoretical way to get her out of the hole. The sides of the hole were vertical, and I could see what Kelly's husband had been thinking with the backhoe. If he could cut a ramp from the front of the hole up to the surface, Bella could just walk out of the hole. Unfortunately, Bella probably wouldn't be able to handle that, even if the ground could. I imagined being in the hole, blindfolded, as something like that was happening inches away from my face. Nope, no way.

My best guess was to get a crane out here and lift her out of the hole. I could easily poke holes in that plan, though. Bella probably wouldn't like flying blind any more than she would like the backhoe digging her out. There was also the issue of getting a crane, and then driving it out here, where we already knew the ground wasn't stable. Cranes are heavy.

It took the TLAER team about thirty minutes to arrive. While we waited, Erica had the owners bring some water out for Bella, as well as her breakfast. The more content we could keep her, the better. We also took some more pictures. You don't see something like this every day.

When the TLAER team arrived, they immediately took charge of the situation. They were a collection of volunteers from various vocations, mostly firefighters and paramedics. In a stroke of luck, we learned that this was a training weekend, and they'd just done a simulation of a nearly identical situation the day before. They were ready.

A young blonde woman and an older man walked over

to Bella and conferenced with Erica. I stayed back out of the way and tried to capture everything with pictures and videos. The rest of the team began unloading equipment from their trailer and setting it up.

The plan was to get a couple of wide straps around Bella, sedate her, cut the edge of the hole away by shovel, and pull her out with a block and tackle. Erica's role would be to administer the sedative to Bella, manage her head on the way up, and then be ready to help her recover once she was out of the hole.

Erica had been hoping to avoid sedating Bella, but there was no way around it. It's always dangerous to knock a horse out, because as soon as they start to wake up, they want to stand up, and they can easily break a leg by trying to get up before the drugs wear off sufficiently. For Bella, this would be further complicated by being blind, as it would be harder for her to regain her equilibrium. Balance and vision go hand in hand, and Bella would be at a supreme disadvantage when she woke up. Erica would have to use a careful drug plan to keep her calm until she could stand on her own. A partially sedated blind horse in a panic would be bad. Really bad.

As the team set to work getting everything ready, Kelly's husband went up to the barn to get Patches. Having her seeing-eye horse nearby would help Bella's disorientation when she woke up and would hopefully help her remain calm.

I had to admire the TLAER team's commitment to safety. They all wore helmets, and made Erica wear one, too. They kept the number of people at the hole to an absolute minimum and talked everyone through the plan so there was no confusion about who was going to do what.

One of the men lowered a wide strap inside of the hole

just behind Bella's front leg. The woman on the other side of the hole reached down with a long pole with a hook on the end and snagged the strap, pulling it up the other side. They repeated the process on the back end, just in front of her rear legs. Once the straps were in place, they hooked them up to a huge block and tackle that was anchored to a truck about fifty feet away.

Bella was so calm it was unbelievable. Erica sat by her head, feeding her treats and stroking her muzzle. They brought a thick, semi-rigid piece of plastic about five feet square, and once the top edge of the hole was shoveled away, they slid the plastic into the hole to make it easier to slide her out, a sort of makeshift ramp. Everything was ready.

Erica gave Bella one last treat, then slid around beside her. I've seen her do some out-of-position stuff before, but this was the first time I'd seen her give a shot in the neck while lying on her belly. Lying down didn't slow her down any, though. As soon as the shot was in, she was right back in front of Bella, talking to her the whole time. In addition to managing her head as they brought her up, she also had to monitor Bella's level of sedation, and be ready to react if something changed.

It took a few minutes for the drugs to kick in, but when the ropes grew taut, I could tell it was time. Erica grabbed Bella by the halter, and the TLAER team began to pull on the long rope coming out of the block and tackle. They went slow, with two people managing the plastic on the side of the hole, trying to keep it in place. At one point they paused, and someone shoveled a bit more dirt out of the way on a spot that was hanging them up. Erica held her head so that it wasn't flopping around, and a few minutes later, she was on the surface. After rearranging her more fully on the plastic, they pulled her far away from the hole to wake up. Then they took the rigging off her and brought Patches over.

Erica had administered the least amount of anesthesia that she could, but it still took a while for Bella to wake up. Once she began to stir, Erica gave her a different drug to keep her calm. The idea was to keep her on the ground until the sedative was completely worn off. This is tough, because horses are defenseless on the ground, and they always want to be standing. It was a long, slow process, but in the end, she was safely on her feet. They brought Patches over, and there was a lot of nickering and sniffing, and everyone was content. It was a touching moment.

On the ride home, I thought about how quickly life can change. Bella rolled with it, despite being unbelievably disadvantaged. Or, perhaps she had an advantage, being accustomed to adversity going into it. It seems like most horses would have lost their mind in that hole. Most people, too, probably. I know I wouldn't have been that calm. Bella clearly had something to teach me about dealing with life, and I hoped that I was being a good student. I also hoped I would never get tested on it like she had!

17

Bored Boarders

We have a staff meeting every Thursday morning at the clinic. This is where we all get back on the same sheet of music, go over upcoming events, have brain-storming sessions, and that sort of thing. This particular meeting involved planning for two upcoming boarders who would be staying at the clinic for a while.

"We're going to need some more bedding," Liz said. "We've got four bags in the shed, which is enough to bed two stalls, but we'll need more before the weekend is over."

"Okay, no problem," I said. "How about hay and feed? Are both horses going to bring their own hay, or do we know yet?"

"There's only one horse coming," Dr. Allison clarified. "The other boarder is a pig named Tank."

"Oh, excellent!" I said. We've been working hard to build our pig clientele, so this was a good thing. "I'm guessing he'll come with everything he needs."

"Yeah, I think so," Dr. Allison said.

"The horse is Sweet Pea," Erica said. "I need you to take the trailer down to Ocala and pick her up."

"Sweet Pea at your trainer's barn?" I asked, making sure I knew who she was talking about.

"Yep," she said. "They can't keep up with her eye meds while they're in North Carolina, so we're going to keep her for a few weeks."

"I got it," I said.

They worked out a schedule for the weekend, as someone was going to have to administer eye medication to Sweet Pea every four hours, day and night. She had recently had surgery on it, and was under a pretty intense care plan, and both her and Tank, the pig, would need to eat twice a day and have stalls cleaned.

I was still at the office when Tank arrived later that morning. He hopped out of the SUV on a leash, and walked around the grass for a few minutes, taking care of his business. When he was done, he and his owner came over to the barn aisle, where Dr. Allison met them.

"Hi, I'm Dr. Allison," she said, offering her hand.

"Hi, I'm Stacey, and this is Tank," the woman replied, shaking hands briefly.

"Hiya, Tank," I said, squatting down to give him a scratch.

Tank sat and offered his hoof for a shake. I was surprised,

to say the least, but I kept my wits about me well enough to realize what he was doing and returned the shake.

"Wow, I've never seen that with a pig before," I said. "That's really impressive!"

"He's pretty refined," Stacey laughed. "He lives indoors, so he has to have manners."

"He seems to handle the leash pretty well," Dr. Allison said. "You must work with him a lot."

"Yeah, he gets a lot of practice," said Stacey. "He won't use the bathroom inside, even on a puppy pad, unless it's a dire emergency, so he goes out on the leash several times a day."

We showed Tank to his stall, and Stacey brought in a bag of toys and a bed for him. Stacey and Dr. Allison went over his feeding instructions and took care of the administrative stuff.

"Is it alright with you if we let him wander around the office during the day?" I asked. "Just so he doesn't have to hang out by himself?"

"Oh sure, he would love that," Stacey replied. "He's very social."

That afternoon, I went and picked up Sweet Pea. She was wearing the pirate mask, as I call it. Horses who have an eye injury often have to wear a mask that has a black plastic bubble over the afflicted side, to keep them from scratching it, and to keep it clean and away from sunlight. To me, it looks like the horse version of a pirate with an eye patch. It's important to remember that when a horse is wearing one of these, they can't see anything on that side. You have to be careful to let them know where you are, and what you are doing, with no surprises.

I got Sweet Pea back to the clinic and settled in next

door to Tank. This was probably an interesting thing for both of them, as Tank had no horse experience, and Sweet Pea probably didn't have any pig experience. I like to think we're bringing the world together, a little bit at a time. They couldn't see each other, but they could hear and smell each other, and there were a few minutes of intense ear twitching and air sniffing.

The next day was Friday, and I went to the clinic to go over some things with Amy, our office manager. Lilly was working the front desk, and Amy and I were in her office down the hall, when the front door opened, and an elderly woman came in. She was short and heavyset, and dressed in her Sunday best. Her dark chocolate skin made the pearls of her necklace and earrings seem to glow.

"Excuse me, is this where the yard sale is at?" she asked Lilly.

"No ma'am, that's at one of the houses a little farther down the road," Lilly said.

I was sitting in the doorway at the other end of the short hall.

"It's the second house on the left," I said. "I went by there when I came in to see if they had any good books."

"Oh, I see," said the lady. "I wasn't sure, and I didn't want to drive down a dirt road, in case there wasn't any place to turn around. Could I trouble you to use the restroom while I'm here?"

"Sure," said Lilly. "It's right there to your right, in the hallway." Suddenly, she jumped up. "Oh, there might be a pig in the bathroom, hang on." She ran around the lady and turned on the bathroom light.

"Did you say a pig?" she asked.

At that moment, Tank came out of the bathroom. The woman's hands flew up to her chest, as if to keep her heart from jumping out.

"Oh, my lord in heaven, there's a pig in the bathroom," she wailed. "Oh Jesus, oh my."

Tank, who is a very large, pink pig, wandered down the hall and into Amy's office. I scratched his head as he came past me.

"Ma'am, are you all right?" Lilly asked.

The elderly lady was holding on to the counter, though I wasn't sure if it was for support, or if she was about to climb up on it.

"There was a pig in the bathroom," she said. "Oh, my lord. I wasn't expecting that. Whew! Did get my heart pumping, glad that's still working. Oh, my Jesus. Well, I need it worse now than I did before, I think."

Lilly was giggling, and I was trying very hard not to be rude with my own laughter. The poor lady shuffled into the bathroom, muttering all the way about pigs and Jesus. I turned to Amy and saw that she had tears streaming down her cheeks and was shaking in silent laughter. That did it for me. I couldn't keep it in, and mine wasn't near as quiet as hers, but I couldn't do anything about it. I hoped that the exhaust fan in the bathroom would keep her from hearing me cackle.

Tank was sitting on the cat bed by the window when I looked to see how he was taking all of this. I already had the giggles, and when I saw him there, with one third of his huge body hanging off each end of the small cat bed, that just pushed me over the edge. I fled the building, and ran out back in the trees until I could get myself under control again. Every time I thought I was okay, I would either replay the poor elderly lady's reaction in my mind, or picture the giant bulk of Tank trying to lie on the cat bed. My cheeks and stomach hurt from laughing too much. Finally, I saw her car creep out the front gate, and I made my way back inside.

Lilly and Amy were at the front desk, both gasping for air.

"Oh my God, I wish you could have seen the look on her face when Tank came out of the bathroom," Lilly said. "I don't think she could have been any more surprised, even if an elephant came walking out!"

Eventually, we managed to recover. Tank was asleep on the cat bed, so we took some pictures of him, and then got back to work.

Tank was super easy to have at the office. Sweet Pea was another thing altogether. Part of it was totally understandable, and that was the eye meds. You can't tell a horse to hold still while you squirt a variety of things in their eye; they just don't have any interest in complying. Instead, we install a lavage, which is a tiny tube that goes through the skin just above the eyelid and runs down their neck. The tube is stitched in place near the eye and taped to their mane to keep it out of harm's way.

To give the medicine, you inject it into the tube down by their shoulder, and then push it through the tube with a syringe of air. This applies the medicine directly to the eye, regardless of how much they are tossing their head, which in Sweet Pea's case was a lot. While highly effective at administering medicine to the place it needs to be, it's also annoying for the horse, because there is a tiny breeze coming out of the tube, until the medicine arrives. Eye injury horses figure out pretty quick that when you come in with a handful of syringes, they don't want any part of it.

Sweet Pea's plan of resistance was to turn so that her good eye was to the wall, and she couldn't see you. I tried to reason with her about this approach.

"If you were out in the wild, and you could only see out of one eye, you would be eaten by a tiger in five minutes," I told her one day. "Turning your blind side to the danger is not a good way of dealing with things."

Sweet Pea didn't care about that. I guess she was pretty confident that we weren't going to eat her. The problem was that it's really dangerous to walk up and touch a horse if it can't see you coming. That's how people get kicked. We had to talk to her so that even though she wouldn't look, she couldn't help but know where you were as you snapped a lead rope on her halter to get her away from the wall.

After the first week at the office, the ophthalmologist came by to check on her post-surgery progress.

"She's looking really good," he said. "I think we can drop her down to about four times a day for a week, and I'll check her out again and see where she's at."

Erica looked over at me, and asked me a question that I later kicked myself for answering the way that I did.

"If we took her to the house, would you be able to give her meds at like noon and four every day? I can do her in the morning and at night, and it would save us from having to come in eight times over the weekend."

"Sure, I can do that," I said. "What about Tank?"

"Tank's going home this afternoon," she said. "Besides, I don't think the cats are ready for Tank. We'd have a full-on mutiny on our hands."

And so I sealed my fate for the next three weeks. Sweet Pea was high-strung in ways I had not anticipated. She paced in her stall, she paced in the paddock when we put her out to graze, and whinnied in a way that was more of a scream when she was separated from the other horses, but she didn't want anything to do with them if they were nearby, and was otherwise a general pain in the ass.

I also found that having to be home at noon and four every day really made for a challenging schedule. It took about forty minutes to give her each series of meds, so my afternoons were basically cut to about three hours. I adapted my routine, but I didn't like it.

It took a long time to give the meds because I had to allow each med five to ten minutes before putting the next one through the lavage. If I gave them too fast, each one would just wash away the one before it. That meant that I had to go in, wait for her to race around the stall a few times and then stand with her head in the corner, or out the window, and then try to get a lead rope on her without her freaking out and accidently trampling me. Once the lead rope was on, it was just a matter of getting the needle into the cap without stabbing myself while she slung her head around in anticipation of the air. Then, step outside, wait ten minutes, and do it again. And again. And again. I understand now why everyone who goes through this will gladly pay someone else to do it in the future. I guarantee you I will!

By the end of the first week of having Sweet Pea at home, I felt like we were developing a semi-functional relationship. I'm pretty good about exuding a calming presence, as long as I'm not already stressed out about something else. Animals pick up on that kind of stuff. If I go in calm, Sweet Pea might get calm and she might not. If I go in stressed, she'll just get more and more ramped up. It was good practice for me on being outwardly calm. Oddly enough, on the rare occasion that I was starting out meds in a bad mood, I found that faking being calm for a half hour would end up with me being all calmed down for real. That's a pretty good deal!

By the end of the second week, I had decided that Sweet Pea was mentally handicapped. She still wouldn't graze out in the paddock, and she stayed stressed out for no apparent reason. She was also very illogical in her approach to everything. Things that shouldn't bother her did, and things that she had a legitimate reason to panic over, she took in stride. Once I decided that her mind didn't work right, it was a lot easier for me to find sympathy for her and deal with her psychosis. If she was being an ass just for the sake of being an ass, then I could be mad at her, but if she couldn't help the way she was, then I just had to do the best I could to get her through it.

Erica gave me some good therapy along the way. She knew what I was dealing with, because she was dealing with it, too.

"Sweet Pea is the most aggravating horse I've ever met," I told her one night. It wasn't the first time I had mentioned it. "She managed to slam her head into my face today and knock my glasses off. Thank God she didn't step on them. I know she didn't do it on purpose, like an attack, but it still pissed me off."

"We can take her back to the clinic if it's getting to be too much," she told me. "I'm really trying to keep the costs down for this owner, but we'll do whatever we have to do."

"I'm just venting my frustrations with her on you," I said.

"I'm not saying I can't deal with her, not at all." I paused for a moment, collecting my thoughts. "I guess what's happening is I'm absorbing all of her craziness, and since I have to show her affection, and be calm with her, I don't have any place to let go of the bad stuff she's giving me. Then when you come home, I'm giving it to you, and that's not fair to you. I'm sorry, I don't think I realized I was handling it this way until just now."

"Nope, don't apologize," she said, wrapping her arms around me and looking up into my eyes. "That's what we all do. It's part of dealing with animals in a positive and professional way, and not giving them any negative attention. I just didn't realize that's what was happening, because you don't usually have much contact with client animals."

"Well, I appreciate you being understanding and forgiving," I said, hugging her back. "I'll work on being a better communicator to you when I need to vent."

By the end of the third week, when Sweet Pea was given the all-clear to come off the meds and go home, I was still happy to see her go. It didn't turn into one of those feel-good movies where the man and the horse start out hating each other, and then become best friends by the end. Maybe that happens in real life, but it didn't happen here. I took Sweet Pea home with a smile on my face, and I whistled all the way back. I will admit that she made our crazy horses seem manageable by comparison, so there's that.

When Sweet Pea was gone, I suddenly felt like I had twice as many hours every day. I also felt like a weight had been taken off of me. She taught me some lessons, but they came at a high price. Still, I wished more than once that Sweet Pea had stayed at the clinic, and Tank had come home with us. At least he was polite!

18

Stars, Bars and Scars

There is a magic time in Florida in the fall when the sun sets early, and it's full dark by seven o'clock, and yet it's still warm. This is the best time of year for stargazing for a guy like me that can't stay awake much past nine p.m. but really wants to look at the sky for an hour or two. One Friday night in late October, we dragged the tarp, comforter, and two pillows out back to the riding arena after supper, as we often do.

The night sky in our back yard is absolutely fantastic. There's not much light pollution out here, and the Milky Way and its millions of stars shine brilliantly on clear nights. This was one of those nights, without a single cloud in the sky. I was checking out the sliver of moon in the binoculars when Erica nudged me.

"Satellite," she said. "Almost straight overhead, going south to north."

I found it, a moving dot that looked about the same size and brightness of a star. It moved at a pretty good pace, crossing the sky in less than five minutes.

The Pleiades constellation was very clear, and once the satellite was out of view, I brought it into focus in the binoculars. Pleiades, or the Seven Sisters, as it's sometimes referred to, is one of the very best things to see through the binoculars. With the naked eye, you can make out six or seven stars in an unusual little cluster. Before I knew which constellation it was, I used to call it 'Gandalf's Rune,' and sometimes I still do, just for fun. With a good pair of binoculars, it turns into seven brilliant diamonds of light on a background of twenty or thirty dimmer stars, and it's just incredible.

I handed the binoculars to Erica. "Check out Gandalf's Rune," I said.

A few minutes later, she handed them back to me. "Okay, I think I found a cluster," she said. "If you start at Pleiades, and go left two bright stars, there's a single star up above it, in the dark area."

I followed her directions. "Okay, I think I see where you're talking about," I said.

"Now, go to the left a bit. It's a little harder to find in the binoculars," she said. "You'll know when you see it, though."

She was right about it being harder. Where there were only two stars with the naked eye, there were ten stars under magnification. It took me a few tries to get the binoculars pointed in the right spot, but I finally found it.

"Oh, that's pretty good," I said, examining the spot. "You can't look directly at it, even in the binoculars, but when you look right beside it, that one star turns into a faint cloud of stars."

"Do you think that's a nebula?" she asked.

"I have no idea," I answered. "It could be… I guess it has to be either a nebula or a cluster, right?"

"I don't know," she said. "I'm not even sure I could find it again to ask someone at the next Astronomy Club star party."

"Yeah, that's the hard part," I agreed. "Nothing is ever oriented the same way somewhere else as it is right here, and it will all be in a different spot in two weeks, anyway."

We checked out a few more interesting spots, waiting for Jupiter to come up over the trees.

"Meteor," Erica said. As usual, I missed it.

"Sometimes I think you just say that to mess with me," I joked.

"Nope, you just consistently look the wrong direction, that's all."

Finally, Jupiter came into view over the trees. It was amazingly bright, and we took a moment to just admire it before using the binoculars. I braced my elbows on the ground to stabilize the lenses as much as I could.

"Okay, I've got Jupiter," I said. "I can see three… maybe four little light spots, so those must be the moons." I passed the binoculars to Erica.

"That's amazing," she breathed. "I can see four, fairly clear. I can't believe that."

"I think that's why it looks so bright tonight," I said. "Everything is at just the right angle to the sun, so they're all reflecting a lot of light towards us."

We took turns admiring it. Finally, while she was staring at Jupiter, I saw a meteor.

"Ha!" I cried out in excitement. "That was a really good one!" The tail lingered in the sky for a moment after it passed, though I wasn't sure if that was real, or just my eyes playing tricks on me.

"I missed it," Erica said, "but I guess it was your turn to see one."

Erica's phone rang, totally shattering the moment. She answered, and within a few seconds, stood up and gestured to me. I quickly gathered up our star-gazing pallet and we headed for the house.

"We're on the way right now," Erica said, hanging up as I came out of the tack room where we store the stargazing stuff.

"I need to put on my other shoes quick," I said, running up the stairs. "What's going on?"

"I need to change shoes, too," she said, following me up the stairs. "We've got to run by the clinic and get the X-ray machine. The Wilson filly did something to her head, and the left side of her face is all swollen up."

"Well, at least we got to see Jupiter and the moons first," I said. "That was pretty incredible."

"Absolutely," she agreed.

The Wilsons live fairly close by, at least compared to some of our clients, so we managed to get there in just under thirty minutes. I grabbed the headlamp and my flashlight, in case the barn lighting wasn't adequate, and we went in.

Carla Wilson was in the first stall, along with a mare and the filly. There was no doubt that something bad had happened; the filly's face was huge and distorted.

"Hi, Erica," she called as we walked up. "I really

appreciate you running over here. I hate to bother you on a Friday night, but our little princess here…" She gestured to the baby, which said everything she needed to say.

"Oh, no worries," said Erica, approaching the filly cautiously. "What did you do, baby girl? Did you run into a tree or something?"

She put a soothing hand on the nervous filly, while Carla held the mare still off to one side. It was a foaling stall, so it was a little bigger than a regular stall, and I was glad to have the extra space. There were a lot of people and horses in a confined area, and that can get dangerous.

"I'm afraid to put a halter on her to hold her still," said Carla. "Do you want a lead rope or something to put around her neck?"

"This is a tough spot," said Erica with a laugh. "She's getting too big to just grab on to and hold her, but I don't want to put a halter on her until we figure out what's going on. What is she now, about six months old?"

"She was a March baby, so she's almost eight months," Carla said. "Although I don't know how that could possibly be, because it seems like she was just born about three or four weeks ago."

"I know it," Erica agreed, turning to me. "Can you grab me a lead rope? We're going to try to figure out a way to hold her still so I can examine her."

I brought a lead rope over from the rack by the tack room. Erica had backed her into a corner and seemed to be having some success in checking her out, so I hung back for a minute.

"Well, even though her eye is swollen shut, I don't think there's anything in it," she said, switching off her headlamp and stepping back. "There aren't any lacerations anywhere either, so we can rule that out. We're going to shoot some radiographs and see what that tells us."

I hung the lead rope on the gate and went back out to the truck to grab the gear. Erica followed me and measured out some drugs in a syringe.

"We're going to sedate her so we can get some decent x-rays," she said. "I'm going to give her some pain meds too, so she'll be more comfortable. With that much edema, she's in a pretty significant amount of pain."

"Edema is swelling, right?" I asked.

"Yep." She winked at me over the vial as she drew up the medication. "Look at you, learning medical jargon."

"One word at a time," I said. "There's a lot to learn."

Back in the barn, I held the filly up against the wall, and Erica gave her the shots. We stepped back to give them a minute to kick in.

"She's really well-behaved," Erica said. "You've obviously been doing a good job of handling her on a pretty regular basis."

"Oh yeah, she gets rubbed all over, and her feet picked up every day," Carla said. "I've seen some wild-child horses that didn't get trained early. I'm not having any of that in my baby!"

"You're doing a great job being a horse mom," Erica said. "I have a few horse moms that need to come live with you for a week so they can see how it's done!"

Carla laughed. "Yeah, it's a shame, but some people just have to learn the hard way. It's too bad for the horses too, they're the real victims when that happens. They wind up at the auction, because nobody wants to try to halter-break them once they're grown, and the farrier can't even trim their feet. It's just sad."

The filly had the drooping head that indicated the sedation was kicking in. We set up the radiograph in the stall door and led the sleepy baby over near it.

"Alright," Erica said, as we donned our lead aprons. "You're going to have to hold the plate with one hand, and hold the lead rope with the other hand, just in case she tries to take a step. Can you handle that?"

"Like a boss," I said with a grin.

We shot a series of images from a variety of angles. When she was satisfied that we had enough to see what there was to see, she stepped back and sat the unit back in its case.

I released the filly and took off my apron as Carla came over, and we all gathered around the computer screen to see the x-rays. The first one, which was a side profile, didn't show anything unusual. The next one was at an angle, centered on the eye socket. Erica magnified the image and traced out some lines with her finger.

"Look right there," she said. "It's not a break, but it could be a hairline fracture."

We went through the rest of the images carefully, but nothing else showed up.

"I'm going to guess that she ran into a tree, or a fencepost, or something like that," Erica said, going back to the second image. "She obviously hit it pretty hard. The skull is thick, but it gets thinner right there around the eye."

"Is that a big deal?" asked Carla.

"No, it won't hurt anything," Erica said. "There isn't anything we could do about it anyway, but she'll heal that up on her own, especially as young as she is. We'll treat the pain and keep an eye on the swelling to make sure it goes back down without any issues developing, but basically it looks a whole lot worse than it is."

"Well, that's great news!" Carla said with a grin. "I thought about every horrible possibility I could come up with while I was waiting for you to get here." She laughed. "I don't know why I was torturing myself."

"Human nature," Erica laughed. "I do it all the time with my guys."

I packed up the gear and took it back to the truck while Erica and Carla talked about treatment for the baby. Once I had everything stowed, I looked up at the sky. I found Pleiades, Taurus, and Orion, which helped me get oriented. I turned myself around until I was in the same perspective that I'd had at the house. I was still trying to find the single star that was hiding a cluster when Erica came out to the truck.

"What did you find?" she asked, looking up.

"Just trying to locate that nebula, or cluster, or whatever it is," I said. "Practicing so we can ask about it at the next star party, but I can't find my way back to it."

"We could always ask James Albury about it the next time we go to the Planetarium," she suggested. "It might be easier there, since he can brighten and dim things, and spin the sky around to just the right spot."

"That's a great idea," I said. "Why didn't I think of that?"

"That's why we're a team," she said. "Come on, let's go home."

We climbed in the truck, but before we could even get out of the driveway, her phone rang again. I stopped, in case it was Carla. Erica answered, and gave me the hand signal to stay put. She grabbed her notebook and pen out of the center console.

"Ok, what's the address?" she asked, jotting down the information. "We're just leaving an emergency, and it happens to be right down the road from you, so we'll be there in about five minutes," she said.

"We've got a face and chest laceration," she announced, hanging up the phone. "She thinks a coyote may have attacked her horse. Turn right out of the driveway. I think it's about two miles from here."

We pulled up to a well-lit barn with a crowd of people standing in it.

"Oh boy," Erica said. "We've got an audience. These aren't regular clients of ours, so I don't know them, or their horses."

"Well, that means we have an opportunity to become their regular vet," I said. Most of the equine veterinarians around here don't see after-hours emergencies, so this is not an unusual situation.

We got out and went in to assess the situation. There were six older people in the barn, all well-dressed and looking a bit out of place in the barn. One of the women stepped forward to greet us.

"Hi, I'm Nancy Short," she said, extending her hand.

I shook her hand. "That's interesting," I replied. "I'm Justin Long. This is my wife, Dr. Erica Lacher."

My joke got a chuckle, which lightened the air a bit, but the atmosphere of the group was still grim. Nancy turned and led us to the other end of the barn. It was a very nice place, clean and well-maintained.

"I really appreciate you coming so quick. Our regular vet won't answer the phone, which I'm not going to put up with. Anyway, we had a dinner party this evening," she explained on the way. "We were out on the patio, when I heard the horses screaming and running around in the pasture. There was also a bunch of barking, but I don't know if it was dogs or coyotes. We never saw them. Mr. Peabody came up to the barn as soon as I turned on the light. I've got him in the small paddock right out the back, here. My husband and son are out there trying to check the rest of the horses and make sure they're not hurt, too."

We stepped out the back of the barn and looked over the fence into a well-lit paddock. Mr. Peabody looked like something from a horror film. His face was covered in blood, and there were flaps of skin hanging down all over the place. Blood trickled to the ground from his chest in thick strings. He was white, so the gore stood out in stark contrast, making the scene even more shocking. I forced myself to maintain a calm, professional attitude, and not blurt out all the horrible things that came to mind, like "HOLY SHIT!" and other similar thoughts.

Erica turned around. "Back to the truck, quick," she ordered, then turned to the woman. "We're going to grab some drugs and some supplies. I'll need a lead rope that can get bloody, and a water hose."

"I'll have both here when you get back," said Nancy. I could tell that she was a solid, no-nonsense kind of person that could handle a crisis, which was a relief in this situation.

We hurried back to the truck.

"That horse is in trouble," she said. "I'm glad we were close by, and not at home."

She directed me to put various things in the tray, as she pulled a variety of drugs out. We headed back through the barn, where the group of dinner guests had migrated down to the paddock.

"Do you mind if we watch?" asked one of the men. "We're all physicians, and this is a really interesting situation for us to observe."

"Sure," Erica said with a grin. "Pay attention, and I'll teach you guys some horse medicine!"

They all laughed and gathered at the fence.

"She's tough," one of them said. "You'd better watch out!"

We approached Mr. Peabody carefully. I stood back with the stuff as Erica walked up to him, speaking softly. He stood still, his head hanging down. Blood and saliva hung in strings, ending in a pool in the dirt. He didn't move when Erica put her hand on his shoulder. The doctors stood at the fence, which was about eight feet away, watching quietly, and Nancy stood by me at the gate with the hose and a lead rope.

"First I'm going to assess the critical structures," Erica said. "He's not panicking, so I'm not going to sedate him, at least for now. I need to see that he can breathe clearly, and if the airflow is obstructed, that needs to be addressed first."

She put her stethoscope on and listened to his breathing for a minute. Satisfied, she examined the damage to his face.

"His breathing sounds surprisingly good," she announced. "He's got a tear on the left nostril, but it isn't adversely affecting the airflow. I'm also checking his eyes here, making sure that they're both here, which they are. No damage; it looks like his cheeks got the worst of it."

Erica lifted a hanging flap of skin. "We've got a pretty serious laceration here. The check is torn all the way through, exposing the teeth and gums."

She continued her examination on the other side, mentioning a few things. The worst of the damage seemed to be the torn cheek, although there were a total of six different lacerations on his face. She checked out his chest next, which also had several bloody spots.

"The wounds on the chest look to be mostly punctures," she said. "Only one of these will need sutures."

She made a quick circuit around the horse, looking for any other injuries. I brought the tray and lead rope over when she was done.

"Alright, I'm going to give him some pain meds and some antibiotics, and then we'll put him back together," she said. "Let's fill the bucket with water, and tear the cotton roll into chunks, and we'll try to clean him up a bit so we can see what we're doing."

I took the bucket over to the gate, and Nancy filled it with the hose. While she was doing that, I tore the thick cotton sheet into squares about six inches on each side, like giant cotton balls, and threw them into the bucket, then carried it all over to Mr. Peabody. Two men walked up from the pastures just then.

"The other horses all look fine," said the older man. "They're all wild-eyed and jittery, but none of them are bleeding anywhere."

"Good," said Nancy. "Dr. Lacher is just about to sew Mr. Peabody back together. It looks like he's going to survive."

The man and his son, who looked to be in his early twenties, joined her at the gate to watch.

I put the lead rope around his neck and let it hang there, so that we would have a handle if he decided to walk around. After giving him the shots, Erica began sponging his face off, carefully lifting the hanging parts up and cleaning around them. He wasn't bleeding freely anymore, so it didn't take long for him to look significantly better.

"Alright," Erica said, tossing the last bit of bloody cotton ball in the pile at her feet. "Now we're going to determine what we can suture, what we can save, and what's going to come off. Obviously the most challenging part is going to be the cheek, but I think we can put most of it back in position, and we'll seal whatever holes are left by bandaging the whole area, so that he'll be able to eat and drink."

I pulled on a pair of disposable gloves, as did Erica. She pulled a syringe out of the tray and began injecting a nerve-blocking drug around the hole in his cheek. When she was finished blocking the area, I handed her the needle drivers and the suture kit, and we got started.

"Hold this in place here," she directed me, as she put a clamp on the strip that was torn away and moved it back up in place. "I'll sew it in place from this end to that end. Try not to pull too hard, but don't let it sag."

I nodded and grabbed the clamp. I held his chin up with my other hand and tried to keep his head at a comfortable height for Erica as she sewed. It took a long time to sew the top and the bottom, but eventually she finished, and stepped back, flexing her hands.

"I'm going to guess that suturing a horse is a lot harder than suturing people," said one of the ladies. "Their skin is so much thicker, it seems like it would be hard on your hands."

"Yeah, it's a workout," Erica agreed. "The face isn't as bad as the flank, and some areas like that where they need more protection, but it still takes its toll."

We moved on to the other injuries, blocking and suturing one at a time. In a few places, the tissue was too damaged to save, and she carefully cut it away. Slowly, his face came back together. There ended up being two holes in his cheeks where the tissue was missing.

"Nancy, if you want to come over here, I need to go over some options with you," Erica said.

Nancy quickly walked up.

"This is all going to get covered in bandages," Erica explained, "but in order to heal, the bandages are going to have to get changed every day. He's also going to need an IV shot of antibiotics every day. If you're confident about handling that here at the farm, that's fine. If not, then we can transport him to our clinic and treat him there."

"I'm fine with the IV shots," said Nancy. "If you'll talk me through the bandaging process, I'll be fine with that, too."

"Perfect," said Erica. "So first off, you need to watch these two open spots, where the tissue is gone. The antibiotics should keep them from getting infected, but we want to monitor them pretty closely when you change the bandage. You'll also want to look all the sutures, and make sure they aren't tearing loose. I may need to come replace some of the sutures a few times, and that's fine. I just need you to keep tabs on them and let me know."

"Alright, that's no problem," said Nancy. "Are these dissolvable?"

"Yep, they sure are," said Erica. "We may end up pulling them out before they dissolve, but we'll see how that goes. We may have to relocate some of them, too. Some of the skin is probably going to slough off around the edges, and it's hard to guess how far that will go before the new tissue begins to form."

Next, they went through the bandaging process. It was complicated, because a horse head is shaped like a funnel, so they had to take the bandage around the back of his neck behind his ears so it would stay in place. When they were done, Mr. Peabody looked like a massive ace bandage with eyes, ears, and a nose sticking out.

"I think that will hold him together," Erica said. "I'll come back out tomorrow evening and do the first bandage change with you, and see what it looks like under there, but I think he's in the best shape we can get him in tonight."

"You did an amazing job," said Nancy.

"Yes, well done," said one of the doctors at the fence. "That was fantastic!"

At that, they all applauded. Erica took a mock bow and laughed. I gathered up all the bloody cotton, gloves, and other bits of trash from the procedure, and made a trip to the truck, as Erica talked shop with the doctors. I brought the bucket back with some chlorhexidine in it to wash the instruments, and overheard some of their conversation.

"I can't imagine how hard it is to be a veterinarian," one of them was saying. "You have to know everything; internal medicine, musculature, ears nose and throat, optometry, emergency trauma, everything! I feel a little inadequate right now, I don't mind saying."

"Me too," said another, with a chuckle. "I do the same basic knee surgeries every day. I really admire the knowledge base you've got to have to practice on a daily basis."

I was proud of Erica for performing and keeping her cool under the attention of other doctors, which seemed to me like a difficult situation, and I was surprised and pleased that the human doctors were so supportive of her. I had rather expected it to be an ego-fest, but it wasn't like that at all. I chastised myself a bit for expecting the worst out of people.

Erica was typing up the instructions on her laptop for Mr. Peabody's care, when Nancy walked out.

"Can you take a credit card?" she asked.

"Sure," said Erica. "I can email you a receipt, or print one out, your choice."

"Email is perfect," said Nancy. "Listen, I'd like to hire you as our regular veterinarian. You answered the phone on the weekend, you had a great response time, and you obviously know what you're doing. I like the way you handled yourself with the guys in there, too. You're my kind of woman."

"Well, thank you," Erica said. "I appreciate that very much, and I'd be happy to be your vet. If you'd like, I can come out next week and meet with you, and meet your crew, and see where everyone stands on things."

"That would be great," said Nancy. "I'll give your office a call and set up an appointment."

On the way home, the excitement of the evening started wearing off, and I realized that it was approaching midnight.

"I am so incredibly tired," I said.

I looked over at Erica. She was sound asleep. I smiled and drove us home.

19

Our First Thanksgiving

Thanksgiving has become an interesting time of year for me. My birthday usually falls near the holiday, but until I met Erica, that's as far as that went. Since then I've learned that something happens over this long weekend, some sort of curse that is exacted upon the world of equines in north central Florida. I can only speculate about its origins, but I can make this prognostication with a fair amount of certainty: between the Wednesday before Thanksgiving, and the Sunday night ending the holiday weekend, at least five, and maybe as many as fifteen horses are doomed to injury, illness, or the big pasture in the sky.

On my first Thanksgiving weekend with Erica, back in 2014, we had been dating for about six months. I came down for the weekend and spent the most interesting birthday of my life riding around seeing horse emergencies with her. It was also a very emotionally challenging weekend, as we had to euthanize three of the horses we saw, and that was my first experience with that. I learned a lot about the life of an equine veterinarian, and it didn't scare me away, so both Erica and I considered it a good screening process, which I passed. It's important to know how your potential spouse's career will affect your life!

Two years later, the 2016 Thanksgiving weekend claimed nine victims; seven of which lived to tell the story. The first call came before the weekend really even got started, on Tuesday evening. The phone rang just as we were cleaning up the super dishes.

"Hello, Dr. Lacher."

I stacked the plates in the dishwasher, trying to be quiet about it.

"I'm headed out the door right now," she said. "I'll be there as fast as I can."

I closed the dishwasher and headed out to the porch to put my shoes on. I could tell without asking that it was serious.

"That was Barbara Evans. Trouper is colicing," she said on the way down the stairs. "He wants to throw himself down and flail."

"That doesn't sound good," I said. I climbed in the driver's seat and started the truck. "They live up by Alachua, right?"

"Yep," Erica confirmed.

She opened her laptop and pulled up his record.

"He's twenty-six, up-to-date on everything, and I don't think we've ever seen him for a colic," she said.

Being the end of November, it was already full dark, despite being just eight o'clock in the evening when we pulled up to their barn. I could see Barbara and Trouper in the yard, and I pointed the headlights in that direction so we could see.

We grabbed all the usual colic diagnostic gear and went over to where he was laying.

"I couldn't keep him up," Barb said. "He's been down about five minutes, but he isn't rolling like he was before. He's probably too tired now."

Erica got behind him, and I took his halter. Instead of trying to get up when we gave him the prod, he laid his head down flat and let out a big sigh. Erica pulled out her pliers and gave him some extra motivation. With a new burst of energy, he made a shuddering lurch, and finally made it upright.

"Alright," I said, patting his neck. "That's a good boy."

Erica checked his gums, and then put her stethoscope on and listened to his heart, breathing, and gut sounds. She stayed on his abdomen for a long time, which is never a good sign. Finally, she stepped back, pulling the stethoscope out of her ears.

"I'm going to give him some pain meds, but I want to palpate him before we do anything," she said.

The palpation took longer than usual too, which is also not a great sign.

"Let's set up the ultrasound machine over by the barn," she said to me. "I'll work on getting him over there while you get it out and ready."

256 · JUSTIN B. LONG

"It's bad, then" said Barbara. "You don't usually ultrasound a colic."

"I want to confirm what I palpated," said Erica, "because it felt like a strangulating lipoma."

"Oh dear," said Barbara. "That's surgical, right?"

"Yeah, but even then, it's not great," said Erica. "The ones that survive the surgery are really prone to terrible laminitis."

"Yes, I've heard that," said Barbara. "But let's be sure, before I start calling everyone."

Erica soaked down his abdomen with alcohol and ran the ultrasound probe down his side until she found what she was looking for.

"I see it," Barbara said, pointing to the screen. "I look at screens like this every day, and a strangulated intestine is pretty easy to spot."

"That's it," Erica agreed. "I'm really sorry, Barbara. I've known Trouper for a long time, and he's not a horse that ever deserved anything bad to happen to him."

"Nope, he's been a sweetheart his whole life," said Barbara, hugging his neck. "Haven't you?"

She stepped back after a moment and wiped her eyes. "Alright, I need to make a few calls, and see who wants to come out. He's really not a surgical candidate, but I don't want him to suffer, so we're not going to wait more than a few minutes."

"No problem, take your time," said Erica. "He's got some really good drugs on board, so we've got a few minutes. We'll go ahead and get ready, and you make your calls."

I packed up the ultrasound machine, and we went back over to the truck to change out the supplies in the tray. I happened to glance over at Trouper while Erica was pulling out the euthanasia solution, and I saw that Barbara was holding the phone up to Trouper's ear. I knew that someone was saying their goodbyes to him, and that almost made me cry.

Barbara's parents pulled up within two minutes, and we walked back over to Trouper with them. Barbara was talking on the phone with someone, explaining the situation.

"We've had this horse since the day he was born," her mother told me. "He hit the ground in that paddock right beside the barn there."

"Wow," I said. "He must have been a pretty good guy, you kept him around a long time."

"Oh, he was a hellion when he was a colt," she said with a smile. "He used to go tearing around the pasture as fast as he could, his little legs just bucking and kicking like all get out. Carl used to call him with a whistle, and he'd come racing over and get a carrot, or a pear. He'd come running, just like a dog."

I laughed, imagining the sight.

"All three of my girls learned to ride on him," she went on. "He was the best cross-rail school horse you ever saw, and Martha did dressage with him, and Kate did show jumping with him. He's had a couple of the grandkids on him too, even since he retired. He was just happy to be hauling the kids around. What a great horse, he's one of a kind."

"It sounds like it," I said. "I'd say you were lucky to have him, and he was lucky to have you."

Barbara hung up the phone, and the family gathered around Trouper, taking turns petting and loving on him. Erica and I hung back, trying to give them their space. After a few moments, Barbara turned to us.

"I think we're going to put him out in the front pasture by his momma," she said. "Dad, do you remember right where she is?"

"Yep, I can find it," he said. "Is he going to be able to walk out there?"

"We'll take it nice and slow for him," said Erica.

We all made our way out to the front pasture. It was very dark, with no moon, and the stars were absolutely mesmerizing. Our flashlights led the way, and we slowly crossed the pasture to a huge live oak tree.

"If you can do it right here, I'll get him buried in the morning," Barbara's dad said.

"You got it," Erica said. "Do you want a minute with him?"

"No, he's suffered long enough on our part," said Barbara's mother. "Let's not make him wait."

"Yeah, let's get it over with," Barbara agreed. She hugged him one last time. "We love you, Trouper. You were the best horse any little girl ever had."

Erica and I stepped up and did our part, and a moment later, it was all over. We drove home in silence, each lost in our own thoughts. I was thinking about how many horses I've driven past in my life, them standing in a field eating grass, me glancing at them, never considering the lives they've led, the lives of others that they might have impacted, or will in the future. I wondered how many Troupers there have been in this world, bringing joy to three generations of people. I decided it was probably a lot.

Three hours later, the ringing phone brought us both out of a sound sleep.

"Hello, Dr. Lacher."

I pulled the covers over my head and tried to pretend I

was dreaming, as I listened to Erica talking someone through the symptoms of what seemed to be another colic. She got out of bed, and I heard her computer start up a moment later. I groaned, gave up my attempts at making it all go away, and got up and began getting dressed.

"We're about forty-five minutes from you," I heard her say. "We'll be leaving within five minutes, and we'll be there as quick as we can."

"Micanopy?" I asked.

"North of Fort White," she said. "Still far, but not as bad as Micanopy."

It was almost one am when we arrived. The lights were on in the tiny barn, and as we walked up, I could see a heavyset woman who looked to be in her sixties holding a horse. She was attempting to turn the horse around and walk towards us, and I could tell right away that she was having a terrible time moving around in the soft dirt. I prayed that she wouldn't fall.

"Hi, I'm Dr. Lacher," said Erica. "This must be Chance. Justin can take him from you, if you'd like."

"Oh, thank you," she said. "I'm Dr. Ramirez, although my PhD is in Neuro-Psychology, and doesn't do me a bit of good with these guys. You just call me Nina." She nodded her head at the horse, and the donkey who was watching from the edge of the light. "I'm so glad you could come, and I'm so sorry for calling you in the middle of the night. This has been going on since eight o'clock last night. I called my vet, and she called me back an hour and a half later and said she couldn't come, so she gave me another phone number for some other vet, and I didn't get an answer, and they never called me back, so I called my vet back to see if she could recommend someone else, and it took her another hour to call me back again, and she gave me a number and that person answered, but was out of town, and she gave me your number."

"Oh, my goodness," I said. "You've had a terrible night!"

"I'm exhausted, and poor Chance is just shaking all over, and yes, it's been a rough night," she agreed. "I'm really not supposed to be out here in the barn, because I'm in pretty bad shape. If I fell out here it could be bad, but my daughter, who always took care of the horses, was in a terrible motorcycle accident, so here I am."

"I'm so sorry you've had such a time," I said. While she was telling me all this, Erica was checking out the horse. "I'm glad you managed to find us. We're going to get you and Chance fixed up here. If you need to go sit down, we can take care of this part."

"Oh, thank you," she said. "I will, just for a moment."

"Let's put him in a stall," Erica said. "We're going to tube him; he's got a pretty decent impaction."

I led Chance into a stall, and then went back to the truck to get the stuff we needed. When I got back, Nina had brought a straight-back chair over and sat down outside the stall and was talking to Erica.

"Usually within an hour or two, they should be back to normal," Erica was saying. "One of the drugs I gave him relaxes everything on the inside, and the water and salt we're going to put in him will break down the impaction and flush everything through and rehydrate him."

She passed the tube up his nose, and I pumped the water into him. Occasionally I caught a glimpse of the donkey, which was outside the stall door in the dark, watching us.

"Your donkey seems to be pretty plugged in to what's going on," I said.

"Oh, she's the neighborhood gossip," laughed Nina. "She's plugged in to everything that happens around here, especially if it has something to do with Chance. They're practically joined at the hip."

We finished up, and Erica printed out the care instructions. "If you have any questions, or if he isn't right, you call me, no matter what time it is," she said.

"Thank you so much," she replied, and gave Erica a huge hug. "You have been truly wonderful to us."

When we finally got home, I was barely able to stagger up the stairs and stumble into bed. I noted with some amount of humor that the coffee pot was going to start brewing itself in another hour. I doubted that I'd make it back up that soon, and I was right. Wednesday morning, I slept in all the way to six-thirty, which is the equivalent of a normal person sleeping in until nine.

Wednesday night was quiet; the calm before the storm. Thursday morning, there was a message on Erica's phone when we came back upstairs from feeding.

"We've got a colic at Sunny Smith's," she announced. "Happy Thanksgiving! Can you wait an hour for breakfast?"

"I'll take a granola bar," I said. "And maybe a hat, since I still have pillow head."

We drove quickly across town. This was a farm I had been to several times before, and I like the Smiths very much. They were both in the barn when we pulled up.

"Good morning," Erica said with a laugh. "Happy Thanksgiving!"

"Yeah, it's starting off great," said Sunny. "Lightning is

just making sure we're thinking about him today."

Erica palpated Lightning and determined that he had a small impaction. "He's got a decent blockage, and a lot of gas built up behind it. We should be able to push it through with some fluids and have him back in business by breakfast time."

"Hey, that sounds pretty good," Austin, Sunny's husband, said.

"I agree," I said. "I'm already hungry, just thinking about the big turkey lunch!"

We pumped some fluids into Lightning, along with some drugs, and managed to get back to the house in time for Erica to ride Ernie before we were supposed to meet the crowd for dinner.

We had an early Thanksgiving dinner at eleven. It was good that we did, because the phone rang at one pm, and we were off to work.

The next one was a paint stallion in Fort White named Handsome. He had diarrhea, and there was a lot of blood in it.

"What are some of the probable causes of something like that?" I asked as we pulled up.

"There aren't very many," Erica said. "The blood and the diarrhea may not be related, either. There's only a couple of ways that blood will be present. We'll have to take a look and see what we've got."

We were greeted by a very energetic boy, who appeared to be about five, and his slightly older sister, along with a dog who seemed excited to see us, even though we'd never been there before.

"Hi there," I said, climbing out of the driver's seat.

"Handsome's got a bloody butt," he said.

"He's got bloody poop in his tail," his sister added.

"Well, we're going to get him all fixed up," I said. "Can you show us where he is?"

The horse, along with two adults, was right in front of the truck, but having been in this situation before, I knew it was important to give the kids a job early on.

"Come on," he said, pointing to his mom. "They're over here!"

Erica talked to the parents for a minute, and then began her exam. While she was palpating him, which he handled surprisingly well considering that he was an intact stallion, her eyebrows shot up.

"He's got two slices, or tears in his rectum," she announced.

"You think maybe he had an itch, and gouged himself trying to scratch it on something?" I asked.

"No, I don't think so," she replied. "There's no trauma at all on the outside, no indication that he rubbed or scraped anything at all."

"What would have caused it?" asked Jodi, the woman who was now shooing the kids away.

"I'm not sure," said Erica. "Sometimes certain forms of cancer can do that, but he doesn't have any of the other signs that are usually present with those. I can't give you an answer on it right away; I'm going to have to do some homework on it. However, the rectum isn't compromised, so I'm not as worried about him as I'd be if the tears went all the way through the wall. We're going to get him on some antibiotics to keep it from getting infected while it heals up, and we're going to adjust his diet a bit to keep the consistency of his poop optimum for healing that type of wound, and we'll go from there."

We did everything we could for Handsome, and headed

home. Erica posted about the case on an equine veterinarian chat board to see if anyone else had run into something similar. He was obviously something of a rare case, because on Friday, there still weren't any responses.

Friday afternoon, I went to play guitars with a friend for a few hours, and while I was gone, Erica had to go back and see Handsome again. I felt guilty for missing the only emergency call we had on Friday, but we made up for it on Saturday.

We managed to get everyone fed Saturday morning, including ourselves. The phone rang about ten o'clock, and we headed out.

"This is a laceration," Erica said as we drove, opening up the computer. "Let's see, the last time we saw Cheyenne was also for a laceration, two years ago. It looks like Dr. Allison has been seeing him for his regular care."

We arrived and assessed the situation.

"Ah, the old 'rip off the eyelid trick.' We can put that back together," Erica said. "It's not too bad at all."

"He's determined to kill himself," Sammi said. "I think this is the third time you've been out here to sew him up."

"He must like the drugs," I joked. "He's exhibiting classic addictive behavior."

"Exactly!" Sammi laughed. "I should have seen it! Now I'm an enabler."

Erica sedated Cheyenne and put a couple of sutures in his eyelid. As she was tying the last one, I heard her phone ringing in the truck.

"Sounds like more excitement on the horizon," I said.

"Take some tangerines with you," said Sammi. "They're ripe, and we're going to have to pick them this weekend. That little tree produces enough tangerines to feed an army."

"I'll absolutely help you out with that," I said. "I noticed the tree when we pulled in; it's crazy how many tangerines are on it!"

The message on the phone turned out to be a colic in High Springs. This wasn't a client of ours, but we had already determined that no one else was seeing their patients on the holiday weekend.

"Is that a common thing?" Ann, the horse's owner, asked. "It seems to me that I haven't ever needed a vet on a weekend before, so I don't know if I ought to be pissed at my vet for not responding or not."

"Well, it happens a lot more than it should," Erica said. "I don't try to steal clients from other vets, but when I'm the one they're seeing every time they have an emergency, a lot of them decide that they like the idea of having a reliable vet that's going to answer the phone when you need them."

George was her horse, an older roan with a smaller roan critter that followed him everywhere.

"I'm not sure what that is," I admitted. "She's the right size and shape for a donkey, but the ears are too short."

"That's Daisy," Ron, Ann's husband, said with a laugh. "She's a mule. She goes everywhere George goes."

George turned out to be a gas colic, so we gave him some fluids. Erica talked them through the process and explained what to expect in the next few hours. We hadn't even gotten the stuff cleaned up and put away when the phone started ringing again.

"It's going to be one of those days," Erica said.

"It already is," I said. "I'm glad we got those tangerines; I'm going to starve to death before we get home for lunch."

Erica listened to the message as we were leaving.

"This one's close," she said. "Head back through High Springs towards Alachua."

"What is it?" I asked.

"This is Bits, a donkey we've been working on. He's got some kind of ear infection, and apparently, it's really bad today. We were out there on Wednesday, and got him going on some antibiotics, but they didn't knock it out."

It was already after noon, and since I'm highly susceptible to becoming hangry, we stopped at Bev's Burgers in High Springs and got some lunch to eat on the way. We arrived to find two donkeys in a small pen in the corner of a pasture, waiting for us.

"The one in the tan halter is Nibbles," Erica explained. "She's Bits' mom. We've determined that they're calmer when they're together. Still, I'm going to need you to try to hold him in a corner, because he's not going to want me to look at his ear. We had to knock him all the way out Wednesday, because he's too painful to let you touch it."

"Oh boy," I said. "Sounds like a good time! Glad we ate lunch."

It turned out that holding Bits still really wasn't an option. I was able to hold him still enough that Erica could get a passing smell of his ear, which was enough for her to know that she needed a better look.

"We're going to have to lay him down again," she explained to Peg and Roger, the concerned parents. "It smells terrible."

"Yeah, I noticed that too," Roger said. "He hasn't eaten any breakfast either, which is way, way out of character for him."

We got the supplies from the truck, and Erica sedated him in the stall.

"As soon as I give him the shot, I'll open the gate, and you lead him out into the pasture away from the fence," she directed. "He's going to go down pretty quick, so don't mess around."

"Got it," I said.

She gave him the shot, opened the gate, and we went charging out into the pasture in a semi-controlled stagger. Despite his small size, he was ridiculously strong. The lunging steps became slower with each one we took, and more weaving and pronounced, and on the tenth step, he fell down.

"Watch the feet," Erica yelled.

"I am," I said. "I'm just trying to keep his head from slamming into the ground."

He kicked wildly for a few seconds, and then he was asleep. I put a towel over his eyes and wrapped it under his head on the ground to keep the dirt out of his eye on that side. Erica quickly got to work cleaning out his ear. Nibbles stood nearby, watching every move we made with her three-year-old baby.

"This ear is a mess," Erica finally said. There was a pile of dirty gauze beside her. "I think we're going to have to take him to the clinic and put him on some more intense antibiotics. They're stronger, but you also have to give them orally, and three times a day."

"Yeah, I don't know that we could get that done here," Roger said. "The other ones were hard enough."

"Donkeys are easy keepers, but they are lousy patients!" Erica laughed. "It's a team project just to get vaccines into mine, so I get it."

"Do you have a way to get him to your clinic?" Roger asked. "And now that I think of it, what do we do about

Nibbles? He's never been away from her for a second of his life."

"We'll bring a trailer out and pick them both up, if that works for you," Erica said. "I'd rather keep them together too, especially since he's never been anywhere before. It's going to be stressful for him, so we want to minimize his stress level the best we can."

"That makes sense to me," Roger agreed. "So, I guess we should get them back in the pen, so we can catch them and get them on the trailer when you get back."

"Yep, that's the best bet," Erica said. "As soon as he's awake enough to stand, we'll get him back in there."

That proved to be extremely challenging. It was a combination of him not wanting to go back in the pen, and his legs not working great. He kept the brakes on, while Erica pulled, and Roger and I pushed. He never really took a step. We would overbalance him to the point that he would have to throw a leg out in front to keep from falling, and then we would start the process all over again. What took about three seconds coming out of the pen took about fifteen minutes to get back in, and I was shaking with muscle failure by the time we got it done.

"Alright," Erica said as we hopped in the truck. "We'll be back in about thirty-five or forty minutes."

We raced to the house and I changed trucks, while Erica stayed in the vet truck, just in case. I quickly hooked up the little two-horse trailer, and we went back. I was trying to get this done before we got another emergency call. There have been times when we had one horse in front of us, and two more waiting, and I didn't like that at all. If it happened again, at least it wouldn't be because I was wasting time.

Erica knew it was going to be a difficult load, so she called Liz, one of our technicians, to see if she could help us. Liz brought her daughter along, and the four of us arrived at the farm at about the same time.

I drove through the pasture and backed right up to the pen where Bits was waiting. Nibbles was in a separate pen right behind Bits. The anesthesia was mostly worn off by this point, and although he wasn't exactly feisty, he was certainly resistant to the idea of getting on a horse trailer. I couldn't blame him, really. After all, he had never seen a horse trailer before, much less been on one. He had never met a horse before either, and I'm sure the trailer smelled strongly of horses.

Bits was in four-legged lockdown, which is the donkey equivalent of having the emergency brake on, and all four wheels chocked. Liz and I stretched a rope between us, and stood on each side of him, with the rope across his back legs. Erica and Jessi, Liz's daughter, pulled on his halter from the front, and Roger blocked the gap by the trailer door to keep him from trying to dart out that way. We pushed and pulled, and Bits pulled and pushed, and twisted and kicked, and inch by inch, he moved forward. I calculated our rate of progress, and gauged the distance remaining to the trailer, and determined that it was going to take us about two weeks to get him all the way in the trailer.

I was running out of energy, having already reduced myself to muscle failure trying to get him into the pen an hour before. Fortunately, Bits was running out of steam too, and had a moment of weakness. His front feet were up on the trailer, and just as he kicked out with one of his back legs, his front feet slid, and his rump came up in the air. Liz and I heaved as Erica and Jessi pulled, and we sort of carried him into the trailer all at once. Bits wasn't expecting it any more than we were, and we managed to get the trailer divider closed on him before he could mount a renewed resistance. We all collapsed on the trailer deck to rest.

"One down, one to go," Liz said.

"I think Nibbles will walk right on, since she's already in there," Roger said hopefully.

I hoped she would. I was totally worn out. Roger got up and walked around to the gate, and we wearily followed him. We had to get her out the gate, around the two pens, and into the trailer. Roger was a bit hasty, and he opened the gate and grabbed her lead rope before the rest of us were in position.

Nibbles was no fool, and had watched everything that had happened. She may not have known where Bits was going, but she was absolutely not interested in joining him. As soon as she stepped out the gate behind Roger, she took off like a shot. We were all tired; Nibbles was well-rested and had a plan. To Roger's credit, he managed to hold on for a few steps, but then he fell. She dragged him a few feet, like a wild mustang in an old western movie, and like the ill-fated cowboy in that classic scene, Roger lost; filthy, beaten up, and lying on the ground like a sack of potatoes.

The rest of us fanned out across the pasture, trying to head her off and drive her back to the pens. I ran as fast as I could, racing her at an angle to the fence on the far side. I managed to get her turned back with a bit of shouting and arm-waving, and we slowly tightened our half-circle around her. When we were down to about a fifty-foot space, she began running back and forth from the pen to the human perimeter, much like a baseball player trapped between bases.

At last, she darted past Erica and raced across the pasture. We started over again.

"If we don't get her this time, we're leaving her here," Erica said. "This is getting ridiculous!"

"We're just getting a second workout today, that's all" I called to her. "This is burning off all the pumpkin delight we ate."

"Good point," she laughed. "But we're still leaving her if this goes much longer. I just got a text, and we have a lower leg laceration waiting on us in Ocala."

"Are you kidding me?" I asked. "This weekend has already been busier than the work week was leading up to it!"

We got Nibbles going back down towards the pen again, and this time Roger was in there, shaking the food bucket.

"Come on, Nibbles," he called. "Come get some food!"

We backed off when she got close, and after a few more minutes of coaxing, she finally went in the pen. Roger let her eat a bite from the bucket as we came up, and waited until Erica had the lead rope before he pulled the bucket away.

"We're not taking any chances this time," Erica said. "We'll both hold the lead rope. You three stand in a row and make a human fence. When we come out, we'll keep her up against the pen, and you fence her in from the other side, and we'll just shuffle to the trailer."

We all got in position. Unlike Bits, Nibbles spent most of her effort trying to run forward, at least until we got to the trailer. We got the other rope across her back legs and repeated the process we used on Bits. Within a few minutes, we had her on the trailer, and the door closed and locked.

"Oh my God," I breathed, hands on my knees. "I thought I was in pretty good shape, but now I'm not so sure."

"Roger, are you okay?" Erica asked. He looked like he had recently been drug across the pasture by a donkey.

"Well, I don't think I had a heart attack," he said. "Ask me again tomorrow when I try to get out of bed!"

We loaded up and drove to the clinic. I backed up to the stall door, and we carefully opened the trailer door. Nibbles stepped off and into the stall without much fanfare, although she was cautious about it. Erica released the divider, and Bits ran out and joined his mother.

"Well, that was rather anti-climactic," I said. "Not that I'm complaining, mind you."

"Liz, I really appreciate you helping us out," Erica said. "We absolutely could not have done that without you two."

"No problem," Liz said. "You know I'm always available for this kind of stuff."

We left the truck and trailer at the clinic, and headed down to Ocala, which is about forty minutes south. Erica rummaged around in the back seat and produced a box of protein bars.

"How about another tangerine, and a bar?" she offered.

"Sounds good," I said. "I sure am glad we stopped and got a burger before we went to Roger's, or I would have passed out and died by now."

"Me too," she agreed. "I'm also glad you got these tangerines. They've kept us alive today."

When we finally got to the training farm in Ocala, the sun was starting to set. Bobbi met us at the barn door.

"He's right over here," she said. "I rinsed the cut off, and it doesn't look too bad. I already called the owner too, and let her know what's going on."

"Oh, it's Wilson," said Erica, shaking her head. "I should have known it was him! I've had to sew him up before."

"Okay, so you know Linda?" Bobbi asked with relief.

"Oh yeah, we're good friends," Erica said. "And don't worry about freaking her out. She knows he's a maniac; that's why he's here getting trained."

She looked at the cut for a moment, which was right down near his hoof. The skin was peeled back and hanging, exposing an area about the size of a silver dollar.

"We're going to have to cut off that flap, because it won't reattach, which means that we're going to have to lay him down."

"You're going to knock him all the way out?" Bobbi asked.

"Yep," Erica said. "I don't trust him to not kick me in the head."

"That's a relief," Bobbi said. "I was trying to figure out how we were going to restrain him while you were working on him."

"Drugs are always the answer," Erica laughed. "Especially with the high-spirited ones, like Arabs."

We went back to the truck and got all the drugs and supplies, then went back to his stall.

"Let's take him outside," Erica said. "I don't want him to hurt himself again when he goes down."

"And he probably would," said Bobbi. "I think he's wired that way."

We got him out and sedated, and Erica quickly went to work on him. She cut the flap of skin off and cleaned the area.

"These heal up pretty well," she explained to Bobbi as she wrapped a bandage around his leg. "You'll need to change this bandage every other day, just like we did with your draft horse when he sliced his leg open last year."

"Okay, that's no problem," said Bobbi. "I got a lot of practice with that."

Wilson began moving his legs just as she finished up with the bandage.

"That was pretty close timing," I said.

"Yeah, I didn't give him a big dose," Erica said. "I don't want to be here for two hours waiting for him to wake up."

"Good call," I said.

About ten minutes later, Wilson was on his feet, looking dazed and confused. Once he was walking around and nibbling on grass again, we headed back to the clinic to feed the donkeys and a horse that was already there. By the time we got home, I was ravenous and exhausted.

The Universe had mercy on us Saturday night, and we managed to get a good night's sleep. Sunday morning about ten, the phone rang again. I was outside cleaning donkey poop out of the trailer when Erica came out.

"Handsome's owners just called," she said.

"Which one was Handsome?" I asked. By this time, they were all running together in my head.

"He was the paint with the rectal tear," she said, "but they weren't calling about him this time. They've got a young goat that's in pretty bad shape."

"Wow, they're having a terrible weekend," I said. "I'm really starting to feel bad for them."

"I know," said Erica. "It comes in threes, right?"

We loaded up and drove to Fort White. When we arrived, the two kids met us at the truck again.

"Max is sick," the little boy reported.

"My daddy said you might as well move in with us," said the little girl. "Are you going to move in?"

Erica laughed. "I hope not. My horses and my cats would be sad if I left them all alone."

"We have horses and cats and goats," said the boy. "We got dogs, too."

We gathered our things and walked across the yard, where a group of people were sitting in a circle on the ground around a small white goat on a blanket. Jodi waved as we walked up.

"Hi," she said. "I'm so sorry to keep bothering you. I know this is getting crazy." She was on the verge of tears.

"My mom is here to help us finish getting moved in," her husband said. He flashed a tired smile. "We can go ahead and set you up a spot too, while we're at it."

I chuckled. "You think you've got a zoo now," I said. "Between our cats and our donkeys, you'd run away from home and never come back."

Jodi managed a smile at that. Erica checked out the goat, which was lying still with his head down. She listened to his heart for a moment, and then sent me back to the truck for some stuff.

"Let's grab the Bio-sponge powder, the small tube, and that giant clear syringe-looking thing," she said. She knows how to speak in terms I can understand.

I took off to the truck, and the little boy ran beside me.

"So, what's your name?" I asked.

"Tommy," he said. "What are we going to do?"

"We're going to get a bucket, and some stuff to try to make the goat better," I said. "Do you know where the water spigot is?"

"Yep, I sure do," he said. "That's where I get the water for the chickens."

I gave him the bucket and grabbed the rest of the stuff. "Alright, let's go fill this up."

Tommy took off around the corner of the house, and I followed. On the far end, he was already filling the bucket when I rounded the corner.

"Man, you're a fast runner," I said.

"Faster than my sister," he boasted.

"That's probably enough water," I said. "Do you think you can carry it?"

"Sure!" he shouted. "I'm big and strong!"

He grabbed the bucket, and after about two steps, had managed to slosh most of the water out.

"I'll tell you what," I said. "Why don't you carry this stuff, and I'll carry the bucket."

We traded around, and I topped off the bucket before heading back over to the goat. Tommy raced ahead.

"I filled the bucket," he announced. "I'm a vet now."

"Alright!" said Erica. "You did a good job, too."

She ran the tube down the goat's throat while I mixed up the Bio-sponge.

"This is a pro-biotic," she explained to the family. "I've given him a shot of antibiotics to kill the bad stuff he's got going on, and this will help him build up the good stuff he needs. We're also putting some Cairo syrup in him to spike his sugar levels and give him enough energy to fight off this infection."

"So, you think he's going to be okay?" asked Jodi.

"It's hard to say with these little guys," Erica said. "Goats are really tough when they're grown up, but the babies are pretty vulnerable to a lot of things. We're going to do everything we can for him, but it's going to be a waiting game."

Once we were done, Tommy helped me carry everything back over to the water spigot and wash it down. Mainly I did the washing, and he talked non-stop, but it was a team effort, nonetheless.

"Alright," I said, turning off the water. "Are you ready to carry all this back to the truck?"

"I'll race you!" he shouted, and took off like a shot.

"Hey, you aren't carrying anything," I called after him. He spun around, ran back, and grabbed the bucket.

"I'll still race you," he said, and was gone.

I laughed and gathered up the rest of the stuff. When I got to the truck, he had already been there, dropped off the bucket, and left again. Erica was typing up the care instructions as I got everything put away.

We were almost home when the phone rang.

"Hello, Dr. Lacher."

She opened her computer and pulled up a file.

"Okay, yes, I know right where you are," she said. "That was Elsie's place, right?"

She listened for a moment.

"Alright, we'll be there in about twenty minutes," she said. "Just keep him in the stall."

She pointed me towards Gainesville as she was getting off the phone.

"Another laceration," she said. "Head towards the north side of Gainesville on Highway 441."

When we arrived, a family of three was waiting for us at the barn.

"Thank you so much for coming out," the woman said. "We've just moved down here from North Carolina, and don't even have a vet yet. We're renting this place from Elsie, and I called her, and she gave me your phone number and said you were the best in town."

"I love Elsie to death," Erica said. "How is she enjoying retirement up in the mountains?"

"Oh, she loves it," the woman said. "Oh, I'm Cynthia, by the way. This is my husband Al, and our daughter, Rebecca. This is her baby with the gash in his shoulder."

She led us over to his stall. "He's been a spitfire right from the start, tearing up everything, including himself."

"His name is Razaman," Rebecca said. "Our friends in North Carolina gave him to me on my twelfth birthday, because the foal we were supposed to get was born dead."

"Aww, that's sad," I said. "It was pretty nice of them to give you another one."

We went into the stall and turned on the light. A young Arabian colt stood there, with a massive gash in his left shoulder. The skin hung down in a large flap, and I could see that the muscle underneath was sliced pretty deep. I used my phone as a light for Erica so she could see what we were dealing with.

"Alright," she said, standing up. "Let's get some drugs and some suture."

We went back to the truck, and she explained the situation to the family as we gathered the necessary supplies into the tray.

"This looks a lot worse than it is," she said. "I'm going to sew the muscle up, and then I'll sew the skin back up over it. The skin is going to die and slough off after a week or two, but it will help protect the area underneath for a while, at least. We really can't put an effective bandage on a shoulder like this, so we've got to do the best we can to keep it clean."

"That makes sense," said Cynthia. "I'm glad it's not too serious."

"Me too," said Rebecca.

We sedated the colt, and Erica used the clippers to shave the hair away from the edge of the wound. She rinsed and cleaned the whole thing, and then began suturing. My main job here was to keep him from swaying too much, take a few pictures, and hand Erica a new suture pack when she ran out. It took about twenty minutes to sew him up all the way.

"Well, that ought to do it for now," she said, straightening out and stretching her back. "He's going to break some of these stitches; there's just no way to avoid that, but there ought to be enough holding it that it will heal up just fine. Do you have a fly sheet or something that will fit him?"

"I don't think I have anything that small," said Cynthia. "Do you think we can make something with some old t-shirts or something to cover it?"

"Absolutely," said Erica. "You have to get creative on these little guys sometimes."

Rebecca disappeared, and returned with some huge shirts about the same time as we finished cleaning up. We went back into the stall. I lifted up his front feet, one at a time, and they slid the t-shirt sleeves over his feet. We lifted the shirt up to his chest.

"Oh yeah," said Cynthia. "Al, grab my scissors out of the feed room right there."

She cut the sides of the t-shirt down the seams. The front of the shirt came all the way up past the wound to his neck, and with another cut down the center, the back came up over his withers. We tied them together at the top, creating a bib.

"That will help out a lot," said Erica. "It will keep it cleaner, and also make it easy for you to access the wound to apply ointment to it."

"Necessity is the mother of invention," said Al.

Erica typed up the care instructions, and we headed back to the house. That was the last emergency of the weekend, and I must admit that I was grateful. Adventures are exciting, but sometimes you need a break from the action. We did get one more phone call that night. It was Jodi, calling to tell us that Max, the little baby goat, had died. I was bummed out about that. Erica did her best to comfort Jodi and her family, but there's only so much you can say.

"It's really hard with the babies," Erica said to Jodi. "You do everything you can, and sometimes it just isn't enough. There's probably nothing you could have done any different, or any better. You're a good mom to your animals. You give them all the right stuff, and provide the right environment, and give them lots of love, and you call the vet when something's wrong, and I'm telling you, that's more than a lot of animals get. It's okay to cry it out, but don't you beat yourself up. Sometimes it just happens, no matter what we do."

Death, despite being a natural part of living, is still a hard thing to accept. My heart went out to little Tommy, who was learning some hard life lessons. Sometimes, that's just the way it is, no matter how hard we try.

20

Final Thoughts

It's a rare privilege to share these moments of other people's lives, and to witness the relationships that they have with their animals. If I'm there, then it's usually a bad situation for them. The experiences that I'm participating in are sometimes the worst moments in their lives, whether they're being faced with making the incredibly difficult decision to send a loved one to heaven or trying to balance their desire to provide the best care against challenging financial constraints. That's a bad spot to be in for an animal owner, and it's difficult to be the care provider too, but that's the real world. Sometimes people can't afford to do what needs to be done, and that's soul-crushing.

In these moments, all the trappings and distractions of life are removed, and the only things that matter are the animal, the people, and the options that they have to help the animal stop suffering. Sometimes we can save the day, and sometimes we can't. Helping people find their way through these events reminds me that there is another side to humanity, and it's the raw side that deals with the really important things, the things that no one talks about, the side that is real and can't be disguised. I like this side of humanity because it's authentic, and no one is putting on a show. At the same time, I hate to see this side, because it's painful for everyone involved, and I don't like to watch people suffer.

I've learned so many things since I met Erica that I can't even begin to list them, and my perspective on life has changed dramatically. One of the things I've realized is that there are a lot of horses out there that have had a bigger and more positive impact on the world than some of the people in this world have had. That can be humbling, but it can also be inspiring. Any horse person will tell you that horses will teach you a lot.

Having a horse is different than having a dog or a cat. I don't say that to diminish the importance of the role that dogs and cats have, because they're important, too. Horses are different for several reasons. First, they tend to live a lot longer than small animals, so they can be part of a family for someone's entire childhood and well into their adult life. The level of interaction is different, too. When someone is participating in something with their horse, whether it's a 4-H riding club or a regional or national sport horse circuit of some kind, they're riding and training constantly, and they develop a relationship with the horse that really can't be compared accurately to anything else. The horse and the person are growing and learning together. It's more than a hobby; it's a lifestyle in every sense of the word. People tell us all the time that they're closer to their horse than they are to most of the people in their lives. The life lessons that they learn in that relationship are invaluable to them. That's not something to take lightly.

Something else that I have learned is that horse people are different from other subcultures in our society. I've been to some really nice houses in neighborhoods where you would expect a butler to answer the door, and the people there come out to the barn and unload hay and feed and stand in the stall and get horseshit on their boots just like anybody else. I've seen horses in the backyards of singlewide trailers that look like they could fall down any second (the trailer, not the horse), and the horses are eating and living better than the people. On the flip side, I've seen horses neglected in both settings, too.

I've seen countless colics whose owner puts on a pot of coffee and stays up all night long with them to make sure they don't regress, or to call the vet if they do. I've seen a woman get thrown off a horse at a horse show and leave in an ambulance, and her friends rally and make sure her horse gets taken home and cared for, and her vehicle's driven home, at the cost of their own horse show experience. I've seen teenage girls who can back a horse trailer around a corner better than some truck drivers I know. The point is that having horses is a lot of work, and some of it is dirty work, and sometimes it's painful, and it's a long-term commitment, and I've come to admire the people who make that commitment and hold true to their obligations to the animals.

I've also learned that there are a lot of people who make that commitment, and then can't or don't hold up their end. In addition to being a lot of work, horses are very expensive to maintain, and I think a lot of people get in over their heads, and get themselves (and their horses) in a jam. In addition to feed and hay, there are other expenses like building and/or maintaining proper fencing, providing cover such as a barn or shed for them to get out of the elements, tack and riding gear, riding clothing, a truck and trailer to haul the horse around, increased hay costs if you can't keep grass growing in their pasture or paddock due to overgrazing, increased water and electricity usage, farrier costs, veterinary costs, club dues, horse show entries, trainer costs, and the list goes on. Love will take you far, but only so far, and admitting defeat and finding someone who can provide a better home for your horse than you can is extremely difficult to do.

The main thing that I have taken away from my experiences so far is joy. The people that I have met in the horse world all have one thing in common, and that is a sense of fulfillment and joy that they get from working with their horse. I think that animals in general fill an emotional need for people that we can't fill with anything else, and horse people have refined that in their own way. Mrs. Cotton wouldn't still be raising babies if there wasn't joy in it, because she has certainly earned the right to stop working so hard if she chose to. It's all about love of the game, and finding your own way to create joy, peace, and fulfillment in your life. That's the recipe for happiness.

I hope that reading this book has enlightened you in some way. If you are a horse person, I hope that I have helped you gain some perspective. If you are not a horse person,

I hope you've learned that there's a lot going on that you didn't know about. So, the next time you're driving down the road, and you see an enclosed stock trailer go by, maybe you'll wonder if there's a camel in there, or perhaps a zebra. Or maybe you'll see a horse in a field and think about all the lives that she might have impacted. Or maybe you'll just appreciate your veterinarian a little more. Whatever it is, I hope your life is a little fuller than it used to be, and thanks for sharing a piece of mine.

Justin B. Long

Justin B. Long is a self-embracing nerd who loves crunching numbers, researching interesting things, and listening to podcasts, in addition to reading loads of books. His exposure to Stephen King's books at the age of 10 probably stunted him in some way, but he is still determined to leave the world a better place than he found it. He lives near Gainesville, Florida on a small farm with his incredible wife, 7 horses, 5 cats, 2 donkeys, 2 dogs, and a sheep named Gerald.